About the Authors

Authors Nora Bryan (left) and Ruth Staal (right).
Photo Jude Dillon.

Ruth Staal, affectionately known in Calgary as "The Bug Lady," and Nora Bryan are avid prairie gardeners who constantly enjoy the wonder of watching plants and bugs grow in their gardens. Embracing a live-and-let-live approach, they share a deep respect for the environment and for the small and not-so-small creatures that dwell in it.

Both Ruth and Nora are active and long-time members of the Calgary Horticultural Society (CHS). Ruth is a co-author of the bestseller *The Calgary Gardener* and writes a regular Q&A column for *The Calgary Herald*. She is also much in demand as the popular "Bug Lady," answering hundreds of bug questions on behalf of the Calgary Horticultural Society and the Calgary Zoo.

Nora Bryan, always eager to share her enthusiasm for bug watching, developed the first bug programs for children's education at the Calgary Zoo. She has written many articles for *Calgary Gardening*, a CHS members' publication.

The
Prairie Gardener's
BOOK of
BUGS

A Guide to Living with Common Garden Insects

NORA BRYAN & RUTH STAAL
Illustrations by Grace Buzik

The publisher gratefully acknowledges the support of The Canada Council for the Arts
and the Department of Canadian Heritage.

THE CANADA COUNCIL | LE CONSEIL DES ARTS
FOR THE ARTS | DU CANADA
SINCE 1957 | DEPUIS 1957

We acknowledge the financial support of the Government of Canada through the Book
Publishing Industry Development Program (BPIDP) for our publishing activities.

Printed in Canada by Friesens

03 04 05 06 07 / 5 4 3 2 1

First published in the United States in 2003 by
Fitzhenry & Whiteside
121 Harvard Avenue, Suite 2
Allston, MA 02134

National Library of Canada Cataloguing in Publication Data

Bryan, Nora, 1959-
The prairie gardener's book of bugs : a guide to living with common
garden insects / Nora Bryan, Ruth Staal ; illustrations by Grace Buzik

Includes bibliographical references and index.
ISBN 1-894004-87-6

1. Garden pests—Prairie Provinces—Identification. 2. Insect
pests—Prairie Provinces—Identification. 3. Beneficial
insects—Prairie Provinces—Identification. I. Buzik, Grace. II.
Staal, Ruth, 1939- III. Title.
SB931.B79 2003   635'.0497'09712   C2002-911423-3

FIFTH
HOUSE

Fifth House Ltd.
A Fitzhenry & Whiteside Company
1511, 1800-4 St. SW
Calgary, Alberta, Canada
T2S 2S5
1-800-387-9776
www.fitzhenry.ca

TABLE OF CONTENTS

FOREWORD

Insects are one of the most abundant life forms on this earth. We share water, plants, food, and space with more insects than we might care to think about. Over one million different species have been named—and who knows how many insects of each species exist—so it is no wonder that we constantly run into them as we share their environments. Insects give us honey for sweetening, fruit from pollination, soil from decomposition, and a clean earth from scavengers. Since many insects eat other insects, they also keep each other in check. But, they eat our trees, bite us and take our blood, and feed on our belongings and food.

It was a pleasure to see and read this book by Ruth Staal and Nora Bryan. They have used a mixture of science and common sense to capture our encounters with insects in our yards and landscapes, bringing together the science of entomology, the business of pest control, and the practical application of having to live with the insects. They have made it clear that we will never "control" insects—there are too many of them and they are too diverse in their behavior—and if we conquer one, others will take its place.

Ruth and Nora's years of experience and quest for knowledge have culminated in this very practical and easily read book. Their pursuit of accuracy and knowledge is evident in their planning and writing. They try to keep it simple so that everyone can understand, and they keep controls practical so that we can deal with the insects we find without harm to ourselves or the environment. By discussing the "good guys," along with the "bad guys," they help us learn to identify and appreciate the different roles that insects play in our yards and gardens.

Sprinkled throughout their writing is a joyful sense of wonder and humor that adds to the quality and enjoyment of this book. Very few books have been written about insects living in our midst on the prairies, and so this book definitely fills a void. For anyone wanting to learn more about the relationship between insects and plants, this book is both useful and a pleasure to read.

Ernest Mengersen
Instructor, Entomology
Olds College

ACKNOWLEDGMENTS

Worthwhile and challenging endeavors are never met without the help and enthusiastic support of colleagues and friends. Indeed, one of the chief pleasures in writing this book was the opportunity to talk "bugs" with fellow gardeners, entomologists, and others. We owe the successful completion of this book to grassroots' cheering of friends and family, expert knowledge of renowned entomologists, valuable suggestions from gardeners, and support from the people at Fifth House.

To Liesbeth Leatherbarrow and Lesley Reynolds, we are grateful for the opportunity to participate in a project like this. We hope our effort measures up to their faith in us.

To Grace Buzik, we remain in awe of the beautiful artwork that makes this book so special. Her talent for making even the lowliest insect a wonder to behold, her thorough research, and her painstaking attention to each detail make this book a work of beauty.

To Ernest Mengersen, we are eternally grateful for taking time from his very busy teaching practice to review our draft manuscript in detail. His corrections, suggestions, and contribution of amazing tidbits of bug lore have enriched this book. We wish to thank Dan Johnson at Agriculture Canada in Lethbridge for helping us understand those most prairie of insects, the oft-misunderstood grasshoppers. Thanks also to Terry Thormin at the Provincial Museum of Alberta for his valuable comments. It is an honor to associate with such experts and guardians of the planet.

To our good friends and gardeners Anita Bianchi, Deb Heap, and Anne Savannah, we thank them for their many suggestions for making this book a truly useful one for prairie gardeners.

To Joe, Nora's husband and champion, we thank him for his painstaking read of draft upon draft, unflinchingly honest feedback, and numerous suggestions for improvements to the text.

Of course, this book would not be possible without the expert support and guidance of Charlene Dobmeier, Richard Janzen, Simone Lee, and Liesbeth and Lesley (once again) at Fifth House.

The bugs described in this book may be encountered in gardens in the Canadian prairies and the northern Great Plains of the United States.

— PART I —

Living With Bugs

I

INTRODUCTION

What do you want to know about bugs? Overwhelmingly, most gardeners would like to know how to control them or make them go away. Some gardeners are interested in telling the "good" bugs, such as lady beetles, from the "bad." Others are interested in attracting bugs such as butterflies, because they are beautiful additions to their garden.

Whether you want to control insects, learn to tell the good from the bad, or attract them to your garden, you have come to the right place. This book will help you see insects as an integral part of your garden, and when you spot a tiny visitor, help you decide whether to try to control it, ignore it, or marvel at it.

Most gardeners classify small creepy-crawlers into two broad categories: bugs and worms. Yet, there is, in fact, tremendous diversity among the types of small creatures you may find in your garden, all of them different from each other. With this book, you'll learn not only about insects, but also about insect relatives, such as spiders, centipedes, and millipedes, and even about some creatures that are in no way related to insects, such as earthworms and slugs.

There are millions of insects and other creepy-crawlers that interact with each other, with your plants, and with the other animals that visit your garden. They feed on your plants or on each other; reproduce, changing from larvae to pupae to adults; build their homes; or engage in a multitude of strategies to increase their chances of survival and multiplication. Many insects are so small, or so well hidden, that you are never aware of them, whereas others are so boldly colored, or dramatically shaped, that you are instantly fascinated or alarmed. You see their signs and how they alter your garden, from enriching your soil to chewing up your prized roses.

One thing is certain. These small creatures are in your garden because the conditions are right for them. They have been provided with the food they need, whether it be plant or animal. They have been lured by suitable mates or have found suitable nesting spots. In short, they have found a great neighborhood. Although you will never have ultimate control over who gets to live in your garden, the more you understand about these creatures, the more you can influence who thrives and who doesn't, simply by altering growing conditions.

Even if you reach a state of harmony with your garden, you may wish to use a control aimed at a specific, unsavory character. This could be anything from constructing a physical barrier to using a good blast of water from the hose or, rarely, a pesticide solution. If pesticide intervention is your desired approach, it is important to understand what you are using and how it affects your garden. Ultimately, however, being armed with knowledge is much more practical and rewarding than being armed with a can of bug spray.

There are thousands of species of bugs that you might discover in a prairie garden—we have called upon Ruth's experience of more than 20 years to identify and describe those that most commonly worry gardeners. We also describe a similar number of beneficial and fascinating bugs, drawing examples from some of the most interesting and conspicuous groups of insects and their relatives.

The bugs included in this book are found in the Canadian prairies, from the eastern edge of the Rocky Mountains, through the southern half of Alberta, Saskatchewan, and Manitoba, and into the northern Great Plains in the United States.

In closing, when you make your daily rounds of the garden and spot a bizarre little lumpy, black, alligatorlike creature on your favorite rose, don't be alarmed. Instead, marvel at it because it is a lady beetle larva, a voracious predator of pesky aphids and, thus, a good friend to gardeners. In fact, most insect visitors should inspire you with a sense of wonder; as you will see upon reading this book, only a very few wreak havoc in the garden.

2

UNDERSTANDING BUGS AND WORMS

Is it a bug or a worm? It seems that any tiny critter with more legs than your pet dog must be a bug and anything with no legs must be some sort of worm. In reality, there is a fascinating diversity of small creatures, many closely related, and a few that are not. In a nutshell, worms are actually members of several distinct major groups of animals, whereas bugs are members of a particular family of insect. Understanding their place in the animal kingdom will help you understand them.

Making Sense of Bugs and Worms

The scientific classification of all living things, the study of which is called taxonomy, was devised as a convenient way of keeping track of all the plants and animals that have been discovered. It also helps you understand the relationships between living things.

The classification in use by natural scientists is always changing as more studies are completed and more opinions are published in reputable scientific publications. Scientists hope that decoding each species' DNA will one day result in a final and accurate understanding of the relationships between

	Classification of Living Things	
Taxonomic Level	**Two-spotted Lady Beetle**	**Human**
kingdom	Animalia (animals)	Animalia (animals)
phylum	Arthropoda (arthropods)	Chordata (back-boned animals)
class	Insecta (insects)	Mammalia (mammals)
order	Coleoptera (beetles)	Primates (primates)
family	Coccinellidae	Hominidae (hominids)
genus	*Adalia*	*Homo*
specific epithet	*bipunctata*	*sapiens*

all living things. Such exactitude is not required for home gardeners, but some basic knowledge of taxonomy is useful and even interesting.

Consider the two-spotted lady beetle (ladybug) in relation to our species. The scientific name of this particular lady beetle is *Adalia bipunctata*, and we are *Homo sapiens*.

Taxonomy may seem intimidating or irrelevant to those who only want to smell the roses (and pick off small things crawling on them), but an acquaintance with a few simple concepts will make the world seem much richer and less confusing. First, note that the classification is hierarchical, ranking plants and animals from broad to more specific categories. Using the classification is like finding a street address anywhere in the world, starting with the country, then moving to state or province, city, street, and finally, street number. Notice that lady beetles and humans are both animals.

Next, note that the accepted system of classification is biased. The phylum Arthropoda, which includes insects and their kin, constitutes nearly a million of the 1.5 million described animals. Back-boned animals form a trivial number of all described species, but, of course, we back-boned humans overemphasize our place in the animal kingdom, and the vast majority of animals that we notice are also back-boned. We are often only aware of arthropods when they are a problem to us.

The last thing to note is that the scientific name of an organism has two parts, uniquely identified by a combination of genus name and specific epithet. Swedish naturalist Carl von Linné developed this binomial system of nomenclature in the eighteenth century. Creatures that share a genus name are very closely related. By convention, all scientific names are expressed in Latin, regardless of their origin. Latin was the scholarly language of choice in the eighteenth century, and von Linné even "latinized" his own name to Carolus Linnaeus.

Most small garden creatures belong to the class Insecta. Some other arthropods of interest belong to the classes that include spiders, mites, centipedes, and millipedes. A few completely unrelated creatures, such as earthworms and slugs, are also important to gardeners.

About Insects and Their Kin

A BASIC ARTHROPOD BLUEPRINT

Insects and their kin, more properly called arthropods, share a few basic body structures that differentiate them from all other life forms. Their defining characteristic is their externally jointed legs—the word "arthropod" derives from the Greek *arthron* (joint) and *pous podos* (foot). Insects, as most of us know, have six legs; spiders and their kin have eight legs. Centipedes can have quite a few

The Etymology of Entomology

Etymology is the study of the origin of words, and entomology is the study of insects and their kin. Understanding the meaning of insect order names can help you remember what they look like. The names of the insect orders are derived from words of Greek origin.

Common Name of Order	Scientific Name of Order	Meaning
dragonflies	Odonata	odon = tooth
grasshoppers	Orthoptera	ortho = straight, ptera = wings
bugs	Hemiptera	hemi = half, ptera = wings
hoppers, aphids	Homoptera	homo = same, ptera = wings
thrips	Thysanoptera	thysanos = fringe, ptera = wings
lacewings	Neuroptera	neuron = sinew or nerve, ptera = wings
beetles	Coleoptera	koleos = sheath, ptera = wings
flies	Diptera	di = two, ptera = wings
caddisflies	Trichoptera	trichos = hair, ptera = wings
butterflies and moths	Lepidoptera	lepis = scale, ptera = wings
bees, wasps, and ants	Hymenoptera	hymen = membrane or "marriage on the wing," ptera = wings

legs, but rarely close to the legendary one hundred. Millipedes may have even more legs than centipedes—but not a thousand. Their bodies are composed of a number of segments; the number varies depending on the class of arthropod.

Unlike vertebrates, arthropods have an exoskeleton, which means that they carry their skeletons on the outside. The skeleton is not made of bone, but is composed mainly of a protein known as chitin, which is covered with a waxy substance. All organs are located within this exoskeleton. The main advantage of an exoskeleton is that it protects arthropods from dehydration and this is is one reason why they have been so successful at colonizing the land.

BUG BODIES

Many arthropods, notably insects, have a three-part body plan, consisting of a head, thorax, and abdomen. Other arthropod classes have fewer or more segments.

Anatomy of an Insect

Three body parts, six legs, and a pair of antennae distinguish insects. Most adult insects also have wings.

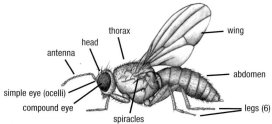

Anatomy of a Spider

Spiders have a prominent abdomen and a fused cephalothorax to which eight legs are attached. A pair of pedipalps on the head functions as an extra set of legs. Spiders don't have antennae, but possess many sensory hairs on the body.

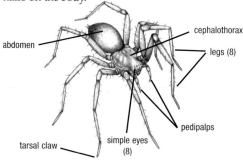

An arthropod's head contains a simple cluster of nerves that constitutes a brain. (It is humbling to think of the diversity of behaviors that can be initiated by this small knot of nerves.) The head, not surprisingly, also holds the eyes, usually a pair of antennae, and the mouthparts, which are quite complex. Some insects, such as beetles, have chewing mouthparts; true bugs, many flies, and butterflies have sucking mouthparts; and some flies, like houseflies, have sponging mouthparts.

Spiders lack antennae, but have a pair of pedipalps, which are modified mouthparts and look a bit like an extra pair of legs. Centipedes and spiders have fangs, called chelicerae, alongside their mouthparts from which venom may be injected into their prey.

The thorax, the middle part of an insect, is the attachment point for the legs and wings and contains the muscles needed for walking and flying. The legs may have a pair of tarsal claws and a sticky pad in between. Flies—well-known wall and ceiling climbers—also have suction cups between the tarsal claws. Most adult insects have wings. Some insects, such as aphids, have winged and wingless generations.

The abdomen is the butt end of an insect and contains the internal organs. There are no legs attached to it. The abdomen of female insects may end with a fierce-looking point which, depending on the species, may be a stinger or an ovipositor. The ovipositor is a tube through which females lay their eggs.

Spiders have a two-part body plan. The head and thorax are fused together and called a cephalothorax, onto which the eight legs are attached. Centipedes have a large number of similar body segments with a pair of legs attached to each. Millipedes have two pairs of legs per segment.

BUG SENSES

Despite having faces right out of a bad science fiction movie, arthropods have senses not unlike our own, and in some cases, their senses can be more acute.

Sight Most arthropods have eyes, or at least light-sensing organs, which are a combination of simple eyes, called ocelli, and compound eyes. Compound eyes are a collection of hundreds, perhaps thousands, of individual light-sensing organs called ommatidia. Each ommatidium collects light from a very specific point, so scientists imagine that the total image would look a bit like a mosaic. The more ommatidia, the higher the image resolution. Insects that see well, such as dragonflies and true flies, have large, conspicuous compound eyes.

Experiments have shown that some insects, such as bees, recognize certain colors. Some can also see ultraviolet light, which we cannot. Many flowers have ultraviolet patterns on their petals, called honey or nectar guides, that direct insects to the nectar source. Some sulphur butterflies have ultraviolet wing patterns, which can be seen by interested members of the opposite sex. In general, insects that see color tend to see towards the blue end of the spectrum; they do not see the color red.

Touch Arthropods use their antennae to make contact with objects of interest to them. Antennae have a variety of purposes that vary between insects and can be threadlike, clublike, bristlelike, or some other shape, depending on the species and what the antennae are used for. Spiders lack antennae but have many sensory hairs on their bodies that serve the same purpose.

Smell/Taste The antennae also serve as smell/taste receptors. To us, the world is mainly a place of sights and sounds, but to many arthropods it is largely a place of smells. Ants communicate interesting finds to nest mates using scent-trails. A male giant silk moth can detect the most minute traces of pheromones released by the female, and thereby make his way to her. Flies can "taste" what they are standing on through their feet.

7

Hearing Most insects do not have special sound-detecting organs, but they can all detect sound-wave vibrations through their bodies or antennae. Insects such as grasshoppers and crickets have well-developed sound-sensing organs but not ears. Most moths can hear the radar emitted by bats and attempt to escape becoming a meal.

BUG INNARDS

The heart of an arthropod is a long vessel that runs along the body and pumps blood throughout it. Bug blood, properly called hemolymph, flows freely through the body cavity, bathing the organs, supplying nutrients, and fighting disease.

Have you ever noticed that bug bits on your windshield are not gory and red? Insect blood may be green or yellow, or even colorless. The red color of human blood comes from hemoglobin, an iron-containing protein necessary for carrying oxygen around in the blood. Since bug blood is not involved in transporting oxygen, it doesn't contain hemoglobin.

Spiders are the true "blue bloods" of the arthropod world. Their blood contains hemocyanin, which makes it blue. This royal liquid does carry some oxygen through the blood.

Arthropods do not have noses or lungs, but instead have a number of holes along the abdomen and thorax, called spiracles, into which air can enter. Air is carried through tubes called tracheae, which branch into ever-smaller passages until the individual cells are served directly with oxygen. Spiders breathe a bit differently. Many spiders have "book lungs" located

Scary Movie! Big Bugs!

Would it be possible for an insect to mutate to the huge proportions we see in movies? To the dismay of many young children, two things make this impossible. First, the exoskeleton, though strong, is not strong enough to support the weight of a super-sized insect. Second, respiration takes place through simple diffusion, which is fine for small creatures, but large ones need a better breathing mechanism, such as lungs.

So, how big can bugs get? Giant crabs, which are a type of arthropod called a crustacean, can be a meter (3 ft.) across because they live in water and water supports the weight of the skeleton. The heaviest insect is a Goliath beetle, which can be over 10 cm (4 in.) long and weigh over 100 g (4 oz.). And the longest insect? Brace yourself. It is a tropical walkingstick, which may be over 30 cm (12 in.) long.

inside the lower front end of the abdomen. Some spiders have a respiratory system similar to an insect's.

A bug's digestive system is similar to ours. It generally has three parts. First there is a foregut in which food may either be stored for regurgitation or be ground down further with toothlike structures. The midgut is where digestion takes place and nutrients are absorbed. In the hindgut, any remaining useful minerals and water are absorbed. Wastes from the blood, in the form of uric acid, also enter the hindgut, joining the solid wastes, and are expelled from the anus.

A BUG'S LIFE

Much of the "worm versus bug confusion" can be cleared up with an understanding of their life cycles. Arthropods have two basic patterns of life cycle: complete and gradual metamorphosis. Certain insects, such as grasshoppers, exhibit gradual metamorphosis, which means that when they are born, they resemble the adult, and with each successive molt (shedding of the exoskeleton), they become larger and more like the adult. The stages between molts are called instars. The immature insects are known as nymphs, or if they live in water, naiads. Spiders share a similar pattern. Baby spiders are called spiderlings.

The transformation of caterpillars into butterflies is a good example of complete metamorphosis. Insects that experience this start out as larvae when they are born. Butterfly and moth larvae are called caterpillars. Beetle babies are affectionately known as grubs, and mother fly's pride and joy is a maggot. Larvae may molt several times, becoming bigger with each molt.

When larvae are ready, they undergo another profound change by morphing into pupae. In the pupal stage, the insect surrounds itself with a hard casing and can do little more than wiggle. Although it seems like not much is happening, inside the pupa the adult is forming, and wings and sexual organs are developing. Many insects overwinter in this stage and the adults emerge in spring.

Insects' lives are usually very short, often terminating within a year. A few insects, most famously the cicadas, may live for over a decade, spending most of their lives as underground larvae.

This basic bug biology is enough for you to distinguish any arthropod from, say, a real worm. Unlike worms, arthropods have legs and an obviously segmented body; they are not slimy. You could be forgiven for thinking a caterpillar is a worm because its legs are not obvious, and its exoskeleton is not readily apparent.

3

TINY CRITTERS IN THE GARDEN

Arthropods in the Garden

INSECTS (CLASS INSECTA)
Most of the critters you find in your garden belong to the class of insects. A brief introduction to the orders and families of insects that are of interest to the prairie gardener follows. Detailed profiles of the more common prairie garden insects are found in Part II of this book.

Dragonflies (Order Odonata) Dragonflies and damselflies comprise one of the oldest orders of insects. In the Carboniferous Age (360–285 million years ago), there were dragonflies with wingspans of over 70 cm (28 in.). It makes you wonder what they were eating and grateful that we aren't gardening during the Carboniferous.

Dragonflies and damselflies are most often found close to water. The larvae, called naiads, are aquatic, feeding on just about anything they can catch. They may live several years as a naiad before emerging onto a reed to perform their final molt as an adult. The adults are a gardener's airborne allies, eating huge numbers of flying insects. They see extremely well and hunt by sight. Prey is caught with the legs and taken to a suitable perch for consumption.

Crickets and Grasshoppers (Order Orthoptera) Members of this venerable order are not usually a problem for urban gardeners; however, they have been the bane of farmers since biblical times. To many, the word "locust" conjures up the word "plague" or "swarm." At one time, a locust plague was believed to be sent by God to punish humans for serious transgressions.

Orthoptera are characterized by their long and powerful hind legs, which give them great jumping ability. Like most insects they have wings, although they don't fly much. Another distinctive aspect is that they "sing." Most grasshoppers are plant-eaters and most crickets are omnivorous. This group is quite well represented on the prairies.

True Bugs (Order Hemiptera) Even though most of us tend to lump all kinds of small creatures into the "bug" group, to entomologists the order Hemiptera contains the true bugs. True bugs look a bit like beetles, but

Grasshopper and Cricket Families of Interest to Prairie Gardeners

Family	Scientific Family Name	Role in the Garden	Example
long-horned grasshopper	Tettigoniidae	minor pest	Mormon cricket (p. 153)
short-horned grasshopper	Acrididae	occasionally serious pest	two-striped grasshopper (p. 152)
cricket	Gryllidae	harmless	field cricket (p. 154)

instead of elytra (fore wings modified to protect the hind wings and body of a beetle), they appear to have an X on their back. The fore wings are leathery at the base and membranous towards the tips, and the wings are held across each other over the back. In between the wings and behind the head, there is a triangular patch called a scutellum. The crossed wings and triangular scutellum give bugs their distinctive X marks.

True bugs have piercing-sucking mouthparts contained within a beak-shaped rostrum, which sounds ominous for gardeners. Certainly many true bugs can pierce and suck the juices from your plants, but many others are fairly innocuous, such as the boxelder bug, and a few prey on other insects.

Aphids, Scales, and Others (Order Homoptera) Aphids and scales are sometimes grouped with the true bugs (Hemiptera), but are kept separate here. Gardeners seldom have anything but bad thoughts about these insects, and with good reason. Aphids and scales suck the juices from plants and may attain large numbers. They share many characteristics with true bugs, including piercing-sucking mouthparts. Other than cicadas, they are all tiny and often wingless.

Homopterans undergo gradual metamorphosis, but their life cycle is a complex and fascinating affair. They owe their success to their incredible ability to propagate. (Stories abound about how thickly we'd be

Bugs In History

Did your parents ever tuck you into bed and caution you with the rhyme "Sleep tight and don't let the bedbugs bite"? Did you ever wonder about those bedbugs? Many bugs suck the juices from animals rather than plants. In the nineteenth century, hardy prairie travelers often shunned inns, preferring to sleep outdoors or in the barn rather than being attacked all night by bedbugs.

Bug Families of Interest to Prairie Gardeners			
Family	**Scientific Family Name**	**Role in the Garden**	**Example**
pirate bug	Anthocoridae	predator	minute pirate bug (p. 155)
stink bug	Pentatomidae	possible pest	many species (p. 157)
scentless plant bug	Rhopalidae	possible minor pest	boxelder bug (p. 156)
plant bug	Miridae	possible pest	ash plant bug (p. 102), tarnished plant bug (p. 157)

buried in aphids if they all survived.) Aphids have both parthenogenetic and viviparous elements to their life cycle. In the spring, the aphids that hatch are all females, and they can produce more aphids without male participation, a reproductive ability known as parthenogenesis. The new aphids just squeeze out of the back end of a mature female and are ready to go. This live birth, or vivipary, can go on all spring and summer. Eventually, winged males and females are born and may fly to new host plants. Many species of aphids alternate between two hosts: a woody plant and a herbaceous one.

All kinds of seemingly dissimilar bugs belong in this group, including leafhoppers, spittlebugs, cicadas, scales, and aphids.

Beetles (Order Coleoptera) If insects are the dominant group of animals on the planet, then beetles are the dominant insects. There are about 370,000 species of beetles in the world, and those are just the ones that have been identified. Beetles are distinguished from other insects mainly by their hard outer wing cases, known as elytra. These are really fore wings that have been modified to protect the hind wings, which are used for flight, and the body of the beetle. The shiny red parts of lady beetles are elytra.

Beetles can be predators, scavengers, or plant-eaters. Sometimes it is the larva, known as a grub, that causes distress to gardeners. Yet, some beetles are useful predators throughout their lives. For example, both lady beetle adults and larvae are predators and valuable aphid controls. There are over one hundred families of beetles in North America, and a few of them are interesting to prairie gardeners.

Flies (Order Diptera) Thinking of flies usually brings to mind the common house fly, *Musca domestica*. But, before you get too active with the

This modified phylogenetic tree shows the relationship between the various bugs that are described in this book.

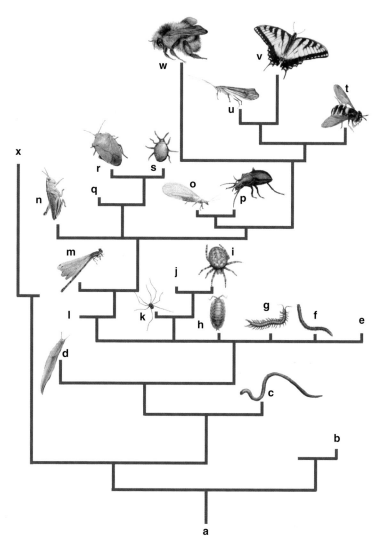

a	Primitive animals	i	Spiders	s	Aphids, scales, leafhoppers
b	Nematodes (roundworms)	j	Mites	t	Flies
c	Segmented worms (includes earthworms)	k	Harvestmen	u	Caddisflies
d	Molluscs (includes slugs)	l	Primitive insects	v	Butterflies and moths
e	Symphyla	m	Dragonflies and damselflies	w	Bees, wasps, sawflies and ants
	Millipedes	n	Grasshoppers and crickets	x	All vertebrates including reptiles, amphibians, fish, birds, and mammals
	ntipedes	o	Lacewings		
	ea (includes sowbugs	p	Beetles		
	s)	q	Thrips		
		r	Bugs		

Homopterans of Interest to Prairie Gardeners			
Family	**Scientific Family Name**	**Role in the Garden**	**Example**
leafhopper	Ciccadellidae	pest	Virginia creeper leafhopper (p. 160)
spittlebug	Aphrophoridae	mainly harmless	meadow spittlebug (p. 159)
aphid	Aphididae	pest	poplar petiole gall aphid (p. 96), green peach aphid (p. 158), currant aphid (p. 126), black willow aphid (p. 95), honeysuckle aphid (p. 97)
adelgid	Adelgidae	pest	spruce gall adelgid (p. 87)
scale	Coccidae	pest	lecanium scale (p. 99)
armored scale	Diaspididae	pest	oystershell scale (p. 101), scurfy scale (p. 99), pine needle scale (p. 86)
whitefly	Aleyrodidae	greenhouse pest	whitefly

flyswatter, consider that many fly species eat other insects or pollinate your flowers and, thus, are your allies in the garden.

True flies only have one pair of wings. Another set of wings has been reduced to a special pair of structures called halteres, which are balancing organs that allow a fly to orient itself rapidly. Flies see very well and usually have huge, bulging, compound eyes. As you will likely know, it takes a real talent with the flyswatter to catch them.

Adult flies might be a nuisance, but it is the larva, commonly referred to as a maggot, that can be your foe. Fruits and vegetables are as inviting to maggots as they are to you.

Butterflies and Moths (Order Lepidoptera) This group of insects often invokes pleasant thoughts of warm summer meadows with happy butterflies sipping nectar delicately from flowers. Unfortunately, your reverie may be disturbed when you realize that this group also contains a large number of "worms" that may crave your garden plants. These "worms" are caterpillars—the larvae of butterflies or moths.

Hundreds of species of butterflies and moths make their home on the prairies, but only a small number of them frequent urban prairie gardens. The caterpillars of butterflies and moths have chewing mouthparts and spend their youth chewing on plants. Although some are generalist

Beetle Families of Interest to Prairie Gardeners

Family	Scientific Family Name	Role in the Garden	Example
ground beetle	Carabidae	predator	European ground beetle (p. 135)
rove beetle	Staphylinidae	predator	rove beetle (p. 136)
scarab beetle	Scarabaeidae	minor pest	June bug (p. 133)
jewel beetle	Buprestidae	pest	bronze birch borer (p. 103)
lady beetle	Coccinellidae	predator	two-spotted lady beetle (p. 164)
blister beetle	Meloidae	minor pest	Nuttall's blister beetle (p. 165)
long-horned beetle	Cerambycidae	pest	poplar borer (p. 105), whitespotted sawyer (p. 89)
leaf beetle	Chrysomelidae	pest	tuber flea beetle (p. 173), cottonwood leaf beetle (p. 106), Colorado potato beetle (p. 176)
weevil	Curculionidae	pest	rose curculio (p. 109), white pine weevil (p. 88), strawberry root weevil (p. 129)
bark beetle	Scolytidae	pest	western ash bark beetle (p. 107), elm bark beetle (p. 108)

many are highly specialized and eat only certain plants, or families of plants. The adult moth or butterfly's primary purpose is to mate and disperse. Once mated, they lay eggs and die soon after. Most moths and butterflies overwinter as eggs or pupae. A few, notably the mourningcloak butterfly, overwinter as an adult in a suitably protected crevice.

Many moths and butterflies use their strawlike mouths to sip nectar from flowers. When they do this, they act as pollinators and become a gardener's friend. Some, however, are so short-lived that they do not possess mouthparts and must mate shortly after emerging from the pupa.

The greater the variety of flowers and caterpillar host plants you have in your garden, the more butterflies you are likely to see. Adding other butterfly features, such as good sunning spots and even mineral licks, helps make your garden a preferred place for them.

Fly Families of Interest to Prairie Gardeners

Family	Scientific Family Name	Role in the Garden	Example
crane fly	Tipulidae	mainly harmless	crane fly (p. 58)
gall midge	Cecidomyiidae	minor pest	chokecherry midge (p. 128)
robber fly	Asilidae	predator	many species (p. 58)
hover fly	Syrphidae	predator, pollinator	many species (p. 59)
fruit fly	Tephritidae	pest	currant fruit fly (p. 127)
rust fly	Psilidae	pest	carrot rust fly (p. 174)
anthomyid fly	Anthomyiidae	pest	onion root maggot (p. 175)
parasitoid fly	Tachinidae	predator	many species (p. 62)

Butterfly Families of Interest to Prairie Gardeners

Family	Scientific Family Name	Role in the Garden	Example
skipper	Hesperiidae	pollinator	Peck's skipper (p. 65)
swallowtail	Papilionidae	pollinator	Canadian tiger swallowtail (p. 66)
blue, copper, and hairstreak	Lycaenidae	pollinator	spring azure (p. 69)
white or sulphur butterflies	Pieridae	pollinator, pest	cabbage white (p. 67)
brushfoot	Nymphalidae	pollinator, minor pest	mourningcloak (spiny elm caterpillar) (pp. 70, 112)
milkweed butterfly	Danaidae	pollinator	monarch (p. 71)

By good fortune, most butterfly families are not a serious problem for gardeners, so you can simply appreciate their beauty. Two exceptions are the imported cabbageworm and the spiny elm caterpillar. The imported cabbageworm, which is the larva of the cabbage white butterfly, can wreak havoc in the vegetable patch. The spiny elm caterpillar can occur in large numbers on elm trees, eating a fair amount of leaf surface, but it will eventually turn into the beautiful mourningcloak butterfly.

Bees, Wasps, and Ants (Order Hymenoptera) Like "wasp-waisted" Victorian ladies, many hymenopterans have an elegant body shape, showing a prominent constriction between the abdomen and thorax. Ants and many bees and wasps live in colonies, working diligently together in apparent harmony, and although not intelligent individually, their organization and behavior in these colonies can be incredibly complex.

Everyone agrees that bees are beneficial because they are important pollinators. Less well known is the value of wasps to the gardener. Most wasps prey fiercely on other insects; for example, ichneumon and braconid wasps are only two of the many wasp families that parasitize caterpillars. While you sip your cup of tea, they patrol your garden for plump caterpillars in which to lay their eggs. The wasp larvae hatch inside the caterpillar and eventually consume it. Even wasps that sting—the vespid wasps—also serve as predators and pollinators.

Ants are generally not a problem in the garden, but gardeners are in the best position to judge. Those who would prosecute ants argue that they may become an annoyance if their nest-building activity uproots plants. Ants may also protect aphids, which they milk for honeydew. Those who would argue in their defense respond that ants turn huge amounts of soil, leading to better soil texture and aeration. They are second only to earthworms in this respect, and some scientists believe that they turn more earth than earthworms do.

The families in this order most likely to cause you distress include the various sawflies, such as leafminers and gall-makers. Sawflies are named for the sawlike ovipositor of the female, who uses it to saw openings into leaves or stems into which she deposits her eggs.

Other Insects A few insects belonging to other orders are also important to gardeners: thrips (p. 161), which are a garden pest; caddisflies (p. 63), which are benign; and lacewings (p. 162), which are helpful predators. They are described in more detail in Part II of this book.

SPIDERS, MITES, AND HARVESTMEN (CLASS ARACHNIDA)

Spiders (Order Araneae) Throughout the ages, spiders have endured more than their fair share of superstition, fear, and loathing. Yet, except in the unlikely event of being bitten by a poisonous spider, people—especially gardeners—

Moth Families of Interest to Prairie Gardeners

Family	Scientific Family Name	Role in the Garden	Example
carpenter moth	Cossidae	pest	carpenterworm (p. 110)
diamondback moth	Plutellidae	pest	diamondback moth (p. 178)
tortricid moth	Tortricidae	minor pest	uglynest caterpillar (p. 111), aspen leaf roller (p. 118)
leaf-blotch mining moth	Gracilliariidae	minor pest	lilac leafminer (p. 120)
clearwing moth	Sessiidae	minor pest	raspberry crown borer (p. 130)
snout or grass moth	Pyralidae	pest	sod webworm (p. 137)
geometrid moth	Geometridae	pest	Bruce spanworm (p. 113), fall cankerworm (p. 114)
lappet moth	Lasiocampidae	pest	forest tent caterpillars (p. 115)
giant silkworm moth	Saturniidae	harmless	polyphemus moth (p. 75)
sphinx moth	Sphingidae	harmless	great ash sphinx (p. 117), galium sphinx (p. 74)
noctuid moth	Noctuidae	pest	glassy cutworm (p. 138), underwing moth (p. 77), delphinium leaftier (p. 167)
tiger moth	Arctiidae	harmless	police car moth (p. 73), yellow woollybear (p. 168)

ought to love spiders. Spiders are amongst the most important predators, feasting on all types of insects.

Spiders belong to the order Araneae, which comprises several exceedingly interesting families of spiders. These include spiders that make webs, that hide chameleonlike in flowers, that run down and then pounce on their prey, and that hide in trap-door tunnels.

Spiders are easy to recognize. All of them have eight legs and two body parts, a combined cephalothorax and an abdomen. A narrow "waist" or pedicel separates the two body parts. Spiders do not have wings, which is a bonus for people afraid of them.

Spiders lack antennae, but have a pair of pedipalps which, although actually part of the mouthparts of the spider, are used much like arms to seize prey.

Butterfly or Moth?

Apart from the sad fact that moths are rarely included in butterfly books, a number of general rules separate the lepidopterans called butterflies from those called moths.

- Butterfly antennae are always (well, almost always) slender with a club-shaped end. Moth antennae vary, but are never like those of a butterfly.
- All butterflies fly by day, whereas *most* moths fly by night.
- Butterflies *tend* to be brightly colored and moths *tend* to be more camouflaged.
- Most butterflies have slender, finely haired bodies, whereas moths tend to be more stout and fuzzy.
- Most butterflies hold their wings vertically unless "sunning" themselves. Moths tend to hold their wings out to the side or tightly over their body.
- Very few butterflies spin cocoons when they pupate, whereas many moths do so. The pupal case of the butterfly is called a chrysalis.

Bee, Wasp, and Ant Families of Interest to Prairie Gardeners

Family	Scientific Family Name	Role in the Garden	Example
common sawfly	Tenthredinidae	often pests	yellow-headed spruce sawfly (p. 91), webspinning sawfly (p. 92), leafminers (pp. 119–120), willow redgall sawfly (p. 121), willow sawfly (p. 122), pear sawfly (p. 122), imported currantworm (p. 131)
ichneumon wasp	Ichneumonidae	parasitoid predator	many species (p. 79)
braconid wasp	Braconidae	parasitoid predator	many species (p. 78)
trichogram-matid wasp	Trichogram-matidae	parasitoid predator	many species (p. 30)
ant	Formicidae	a controversial character	many species (p. 139)
vespid wasp	Vespidae	predator	yellowjacket (p. 81)
leafcutter bee	Megachilidae	pollinator	many species (p. 169)
bumblebee and honeybee	Apidae	pollinator	many species (p. 83)

Beware!

Most creatures, from humans to birds, learn early on that buzzing black-and-yellow-striped insects are to be avoided, or the consequences are painful. Indeed, vespid wasps can be aggressive, but many other insects have also adopted this coloring and demeanor to fool potential predators. Clearwing moths and hover flies are two examples of insects that make use of this clever ruse.

Male spiders also use their pedipalps as sex organs; they charge the ends of them with sperm from an opening on their abdomen, and when mating, insert them into the female spider's genital opening, the epigynum. Sex can be very interesting in the arthropod world.

Despite our worst fears about spiders, they do not bite. The business ends of their mouthparts, called chelicerae, are hollow fangs, which are used to pierce and inject venom to kill or paralyze their prey. In addition to venom, spiders also inject digestive enzymes to liquefy the prey's innards, making them easy to suck. If that doesn't make you feel better about spiders, you can be comforted by the fact that very few of them are dangerous to humans. On the prairies, it is possible to encounter a black widow spider, but it is quite shy, not that common, and its "bites" are rarely fatal. Don't worry, you are still at the top of the food chain.

Most spiders have eight simple eyes. Although many do not see particularly well, some, such as jumping spiders, have very good vision. If you see one and get the impression it is watching you, it probably is—jumping spiders are very curious.

Mites (Order Acarina) Like spiders, mites have eight legs, pedipalps, and chelicerae, but unlike spiders, they only have one discernable body part. This order contains species that may harm your beloved garden plants, yet they are so small that their presence usually is only known by the leaf damage they cause and the very fine silken threads that are visible when misted with water.

Some mites are beneficial, preying on aphids, soil roundworms (nematodes), and other undesirables. However, the spider mite family (Tetranychidae) contains the plant-juice-sucking scourges of both outdoor and indoor plants.

Harvestmen (Order Opiliones) Harvestmen, also called daddy longlegs, have an obvious resemblance to spiders, but differ in some important ways. Although they have an abdomen and a cephalothorax, they seem to have only one roundish or oblong body part. They have eight legs, but the legs are quite delicate and often break off. They have two eyes on short stalks. Harvestmen do not spin silk.

Spider Love Life

Like all titillating tales, a spider's love life can be a tricky affair, fraught with disappointments and dangerous adventures. Female spiders have a reputation for surliness, if not downright aggressiveness, towards the males of their species. This reputation is not unwarranted. The males of a large number of species must approach a female with caution and must give her all the right signals before she accepts him as a mate instead of a meal. For example:

- A male web-spinning spider usually plucks the female's web to advertise his intent before he gets too close.
- A male jumping spider must do some elaborate signaling with his legs, semaphore-fashion, before the female is impressed.
- In some cases, the male is so small that the female does not even acknowledge him.
- A male crab spider doesn't bother with niceties; he throws some silk over the female to restrain her during mating.
- A male long-jawed orb weaver holds the female's fangs open during mating.

Despite all this, some spiders do form fairly congenial matrimonial relationships, such as the American house spider (*Achaearanea tepidariorum*). The period just after mating is another dangerous time for male spiders as female spiders lose interest in their mates quickly and go back to their main occupations of hunting and eating. Some males orient themselves during mating so that they have a good chance of escaping in time. Others seem to willingly offer up their bodies as food for their mate. Talk about dying for love.

For some peculiar reason, these creatures are usually found around house foundations. Like spiders, they are predators and are therefore your friends.

MULTI-LEGGED GARDEN ARTHROPODS

As a prairie gardener, you can find representatives of the remaining arthropod classes in your garden, including centipedes (Class Chilopoda), millipedes (Class Diplopoda), symphylans (Class Symphyla), and even crustaceans (Class Crustacea) in the shape of sowbugs. They share the basic characteristics of all arthropods, namely, a hard exoskeleton and jointed legs. Centipedes, millipedes, and symphylans are often grouped together in the superfamily Myriapoda.

Although they are not that closely related to insects or to each other, these arthropods all have multiple legs and longish bodies with many segments, and can generally be found hiding in damp, dark places. With

Spider Families of Interest to Prairie Gardeners			
Family	**Scientific Family Name**	**Role in the Garden**	**Example**
orb-web weaver	Araneidae	predator	jewel spider (p. 180)
long-jawed orb-web weaver	Tetragnathidae	predator	long-jawed orb-weaver (p. 181)
funnel-web weaver	Agelenidae	predator	house spider (p. 185)
cobweb weaver	Theridiidae	predator	black widow spider (p. 185)
sheet-web weaver	Linyphiidae	predator	many species (p. 183)
crab spider	Thomisidae	predator, hides in flowers	goldenrod crab spider (p. 173)
jumping spider	Salticidae	predator, stalks and pounces on prey	many species (p. 170)
wolf spider	Lycosidae	predator, ground hunter	many species (p. 145)

the exception of symphylans, which may damage plant roots, most myriapods are your allies. Centipedes are efficient predators, while millipedes and sowbugs stick to the essential task of processing decaying vegetable matter into good soil.

Non-arthropods in the Garden

EARTHWORMS (PHYLUM ANNELIDA, ORDER OLIGOCHAETA, FAMILY LUMBRICIDAE)

If various insect larvae are not really worms, then what is? Although many phyla are commonly known as worms of one kind or another, it is lumbricid worms, commonly called earthworms, that are of interest to gardeners. Earthworms are a relatively small family of legless creatures in the phylum Annelida (segmented worms). Most of the worms in this large phylum are strange bristly creatures that live in the ocean, far from the hearts and minds of gardeners.

Lovable prairie earthworms have soft bodies with some backward-facing bristles, called chaetae, that are hard to see. These bristles anchor the worms to the inside of their burrows, which comes in handy when a hungry robin tries to pull them out. Worms have a mouth at the front and an anus at the back.

All earthworms make their living by moving through the earth, digesting various amounts of vegetable and mineral matter, and turning it into good soil, which is the foundation for healthy plants. As far as your plants are concerned, there is no such thing as a bad worm. Some of the larger worms may bring clay up to the surface and deposit it on your lawn, giving it a lumpy texture, but this is purely an aesthetic or comfort issue. It is actually beneficial because the lawn is being aerated in the process.

SLUGS (PHYLUM MOLLUSCA, CLASS GASTROPODA)

If earthworms are the gardener's "yin" in the world of legless creatures, then slugs are the "yang." From a gardener's perspective, slugs are a curse. Basically shell-less snails, they have a soft, mucous-covered body, with a pair of tentacles on the head. Slugs have rasping mouthparts called radulae and feed by rasping away at the leaves and stems of your garden treasures. They prefer moist environments with cover, such as well-mulched beds.

Slugs are a nutritious food for many prairie birds, so your measures for controlling slugs should not harm your avian friends. Fortunately, there are safe slug baits on the market and other homemade remedies that are effective.

4

A GARDEN YOU CAN LIVE IN

You might as well face it: your garden is never going to be like your living room. Hundreds of thousands, if not millions, of small, wiggly organisms live in your garden, in the air, on your plants, and in your soil. Instead of an "outdoor living room with plants," think of your garden as a habitat within an urban ecosystem. It is a refuge, not only for you, but also for birds, small mammals, maybe even reptiles and amphibians, and, of course, the countless insects, spiders, worms, and others that are attracted to the habitat you have crafted.

Most organisms are not a problem for you or your plants and, in fact, are necessary for the overall health of your garden. Of course, certain critters may get out of hand and threaten to destroy some of your carefully grown treasures. But, before you bring out the bug spray, there are a number of things you can do to make your garden habitat a place where, for the most part, everyone can exist peaceably and in balance.

Know Thine Enemy

The most important thing you can arm yourself with is knowledge. Become familiar with the bugs in your garden and learn to recognize the few that might be a problem before your plants disappear before your very eyes.

The most problematic bugs are species that have been introduced into the environment, either accidentally or deliberately. In a natural ecosystem, predators regulate the populations of other animals. However, when species are introduced to areas where their enemies are absent, they may flourish without restraint. Imported currantworm, imported cabbageworm, and European elm bark beetle are some of the better known evildoers on the prairies.

Plan a Balanced Garden

A well-balanced garden brings to mind an aesthetic arrangement of tall and short plantings, strategically placed features, and a well-thought-out color scheme. Although these ideas are important for creating a pleasant garden, the notion of balance can also refer to a well-balanced habitat. You can incorporate elements into your landscape that will accomplish this. For example, choose a wide variety of plants, avoid plants that are vulnerable to bugs, grow strong plants, and maintain healthy soil.

GROW A VARIETY OF PLANTS

Having a large variety of plants in the garden may not strike you as a deliberate approach for avoiding pest problems, but it is one of the best strategies at your disposal. Many potential pest species are host specific, feeding only on one or a few select plants.

Large areas of the same plant, such as some replanted forests and agricultural crops (called monocultures), are more susceptible to pest problems than a garden is. Individual pests may proliferate wildly in the presence of an unnatural bounty of their favorite food. One benefit of varied planting is that you attract a greater variety of birds and beneficial insects.

Choose a variety of trees and shrubs that are not closely related. Plant similar plants in separate parts of the garden, further reducing the chances that a potential pest will find all of your treasures. For example, currant shrubs may be defoliated rather rapidly by the imported currantworm, but having these shrubs in different parts of your garden reduces the chances that they are all defoliated, should you fail to spot the invaders in a timely manner. A similar strategy can be used with vegetable crops.

AVOID BUG MAGNETS

An obvious strategy is to avoid plants that seem prone to bug infestations, year after year. For example, Virginia creeper is very susceptible to damage by leafhoppers. The leafhoppers rarely kill the plant, but they do detract significantly from its appearance, which is the main reason for planting such a vine in the first place. To avoid this problem, consider alternatives such as clematis. Also, look for pest-resistant cultivars when choosing plants for your garden.

GROW STRONG PLANTS

Plants have a much greater chance of withstanding insect infestation if they are in good condition, as they have lots of reserves and can spare a few leaves and vital juices.

Choose plants suitable for the microclimates in your garden. For example, sun-loving plants should be in a south-facing exposure. Plants that like their roots well drained should not be in a boggy or a clay-dense area of the garden. Then, water and fertilize your plants appropriately. Prune trees properly and clean tree wounds.

PROVIDE A GOOD SOIL FOUNDATION

As well as being a place to anchor plants and a source of nutrients, soil is also an important habitat for many of the small creatures in your garden. Wanted and unwanted, they make their home in soil, under rocks, or amongst leaf mold. There is nothing you can, or should, do about it. Healthy soil contains a huge diversity of bugs, fungi, and bacteria, and the wars waged between the good, the bad, and the ugly continue night and day. All you need to do is avoid contaminating your soil with pesticides and disturb it as little as practical.

Add compost to your soil to improve its texture and provide important nutrients for plants; in doing so, you also provide food for worms. Worms can't make good soil out of bad, but if they have organic matter to eat, they will surely rise to their full potential.

Permanent and winter mulches are overwhelmingly beneficial, especially in a dry, windy prairie garden, but mulches can also harbor slugs and other undesirables. Use slug baits or pull mulches away from those plants in which slugs seem to delight.

In vegetable gardens, turning the soil in the fall to expose overwintering vegetable pests is a worthwhile exercise. Crop rotation in vegetable gardens is also a time-honored and valuable measure for pest control.

Use Cultural Controls

Despite being well-balanced, your garden might still attract more tiny creatures than you would like. Before you reach for the spray, first try some of these powerful tools—the hose, handpicking, pruning, physical barriers, and biologicals.

THE HOSE, THE WHOLE HOSE, AND NOTHING BUT THE HOSE

Although you bought a hose with a nozzle to keep your garden treasures well watered, you should also consider it as your first and foremost weapon against identified pests such as aphids and leafhoppers. A well-aimed burst of water on plagued plants, every few days, may be all you need for bug control.

Certain bugs, such as spider mites, thrive in hot, dry conditions, and spraying plants prone to spider mite during the dog days of summer may circumvent an infestation.

If you use contact insecticides, including insecticidal soap, spray your plants down when the insecticide has done its job. Plants don't like coatings on their leaves, and such residues should be washed off, especially during hot, dry conditions.

HANDPICKING AND PRUNING

Handpicking insect pests is like exercise—you wish there was an easier way. However, the most effective way to battle some of the larger plant munchers, such as slugs and caterpillars, is to physically remove them. Wear gloves or use tweezers if you have to. If you are too squeamish to squish them, remove the affected plant stems or tips, bugs and all. Alternatively, drown the culprits in a bucket of very hot or soapy water, or throw them out in the alleyway or up on the garage roof where birds will find them.

A useful technique for managing bugs that attack a tree from within, such as white pine weevil or elm bark beetles, is to carefully prune the affected branches and dispose of them in the garbage.

BARRIERS

Various physical barriers are effective for keeping bugs from getting to tender plants. Barriers are especially useful in vegetable gardens where aesthetics are less important than keeping the harvest for human consumption.

Floating Row Covers Especially designed for vegetable rows, these lightweight covers of spun polyester or other porous materials let in air, light, and water, but exclude insects. Cover plants with enough slack to allow for growth, and secure the row covers around the edges with rocks, bricks, soil, or any handy, heavy object.

Collars Collars prevent crawling organisms from reaching the base of tender plants or seedlings; they are particularly effective against cutworms. Construct collars by cutting old plastic flowerpots or plastic bottles crosswise into sturdy rings. Place them around seedlings and push them into the soil to a depth of a few centimeters (about an inch), or bugs may burrow beneath them.

Copper Rings or Barriers Copper rings or barriers are effective against slugs. Slugs avoid metal since it gives them an unpleasant shock. Copper sheeting, copper, foil, and copper tape are available from garden centers, electrical supply stores, or hobby stores catering to stained-glass arts.

Rings can be fashioned from copper sheeting and placed around susceptible plants. Be sure no leaves touch the ground outside the ring, or slugs will just use them as a bridge. Copper foil or tape can be stapled or nailed to wooden barriers or taped around the edge of juicy container plants.

Diatomaceous Earth Diatomaceous earth, formed from the ground shells of marine plankton called diatoms, is very sharp and abrasive. A sprinkling around the base of tender plants is a veritable minefield to soft-bodied crawlers, which suffer cuts to the body and eventually die of dehydration.

BAIT

Baits tempt bugs to their doom. The temptation might be poison cleverly disguised as food or fake chemical "come-ons" from members of the opposite sex. The things we do to trick the little fellas.

Slug Bait The new slug baits on the market are very safe for people and pets, but are lethal to slugs. Slugs are attracted to the poisoned bait, feed, and then die in a couple of days. This bait is usually pelletized; sprinkle it according to the directions on the package.

Yellow Sticky Cards This ruse makes use of the fact that some insects are irresistibly attracted to the color yellow. Yellow sticky cards are best used in a house or greenhouse to avoid accidentally trapping bees and other good bugs outside.

Pheromone Traps These new high-tech baits are a siren call, wafting sex pheromones to lure unsuspecting male insects. Since each insect produces its own distinctive pheromones, you must know your foe and purchase a trap designed specifically for it. These traps tend to be expensive and can attract insects to places where they might not have gone of their own accord. They are usually employed commercially to measure the abundance of certain species rather than to eliminate them. They are not practical for the average gardener.

BIOLOGICALS

To make the best use of the fact that bugs eat bugs, cultivate a well-balanced garden and avoid pesticides. Then, predators will come. However, as more about arthropod life cycles is known, and as more gardeners look for bug control measures other than pesticides, various predators or parasites are offered for sale. These organisms are called biological controls, or biologicals for short. Purchased biologicals are best used in indoor areas such as greenhouses where they can be forced to stay where you want them. Additionally, many biologicals need the warmer and more humid conditions found in a greenhouse.

Outdoors, purchased biologicals can be of some help if deployed properly and if they accept your invitation of a new home—but those are big "ifs." A very common outcome is that they disperse without doing what you had hoped. At worst, they could be non-native species that may compete against natives with unintended consequences over time. For example, there is emerging evidence that our native transverse lady beetle is being out-competed by, or hybridizing with, the larger, non-native seven-spotted lady beetle. Whether this is a bad or merely insignificant outcome is unknown, but in general, reduction in native species diversity is not a good thing.

Biological controls are not always insects. Microbial pesticides (fungi, viruses, or bacteria) are becoming a common choice for gardeners who do not want to contaminate the air, water, and soil. Microbials can be very effective, and they have the added advantage of targeting specific victims. A very effective measure against the caterpillars of butterflies and moths is the bacteria *Bacillus thuringiensis* var. *kurstaki* (BTk); other varieties of BT can be used against other insects. However, as is true of everything in life, this is not a "silver bullet." The drawback of using microbials is that insects can develop immunities to them. Do not use them carelessly or as a preventative measure.

Nematodes are another biological control. Nematoda, or roundworm, is a huge phylum of parasitic, microscopic worms (not related to earthworms). Billions of nematodes live everywhere, including within our own bodies. For every living thing on earth there probably is a specific nematode that will parasitize it. Some nematodes are agricultural or garden pests, damaging certain plants with their parasitic actions. You can trump these pests by introducing other nematodes that parasitize the parasite.

If you decide to purchase biologicals, especially over the Internet, first ask yourself the following questions:

- Can I afford wasting money if the "cure" does not work or does its work elsewhere?

- If I am importing, have I factored in the cost of permits? Are the organisms even permitted in my country?

- Will the control work in my garden conditions? Can I provide the correct humidity and temperature?

- Am I contributing to the introduction of a non-native species that may become a future problem?

ENLIST THE HELP OF YOUR CHILDREN

If you have children, consider their special talents. Creepy-crawlers endlessly fascinate many children, whose boundless enthusiasm, combined with their short stature and keen eyesight, make them excellent bug spotters. Make it a game to find as many bugs as possible in your garden, including eggs under leaves. Once the quarry is spotted, use a book like this one to see what kind of role it plays in your garden. Consider keeping unknown eggs, larvae, or pupae, with their suspected food plant, in jars or terraria outdoors until they develop fully. Both you and your children will learn about the lives being lived in your garden, and how to spot the troublemakers before they become full grown.

Some Common Biological Controls		
Predator	**Victim**	**Notes**
predatory mites, e.g., *Phytoseiulus persimilis*	pest mites and thrips	use indoors or in greenhouse
seven-spotted lady beetle	aphids	not native to the prairies, thus may displace native lady beetles; no guarantee they will stay
trichogrammatid wasps	caterpillar eggs	use indoors or in greenhouse
nematodes	thrips, fungus gnat larvae, other organisms	need suitable soil conditions and temperatures
aphidius wasps	aphids	use indoors or in greenhouse
aphidoletes midge	aphids	use indoors or in greenhouse
minute pirate bug (*Orius* spp.)	aphids, thrips, mites, small caterpillars	use indoors or in greenhouse
green lacewing	caterpillars, scales, aphids,spider mites, mealy bugs	use indoors or in greenhouse; attacks a variety of pests
praying mantis	whatever insects it can catch	not a prairie native, unlikely to overwinter; not proven effective; eats good bugs too; fun for kids

LIVE AND LET LIVE

There is one final thing that you can do when faced with unusual small creatures of dubious design, and that is to live with them. It sounds simple enough, but we have been conditioned in modern times to sanitize our surroundings. Consider that things may be okay just the way they are. Nature adjusts to the comings and goings of various populations of critters and you can decide to do the same.

5

DIAGNOSING TROUBLE

B ugs are blamed for an incredible number of problems—and sometimes they deserve it—but they certainly don't cause all the holes in plant leaves or the many other curious or worrisome things that can send you scurrying for a pesticide. Indeed, far too many plants and trees are sprayed with insecticides when there are no bugs there at all. Fungi, viruses, bacteria, and even the effects of weather can also cause leaf, trunk, or flower damage. By asking yourself a few important questions and making simple observations, you can make an educated diagnosis of what is ailing your plants and determine an appropriate course of action.

Identifying the Problem

If you were ill, your doctor would ask you a series of questions before making a diagnosis. Do the same for your plants. Before choosing your method of attack, make sure you have identified the problem. Ask yourself the following questions.

- What symptoms are causing concern (see table on pp. 33–35)?
- Is it getting worse from day to day, or is it the same as when I first noticed it?
- Where could an insect be? Look under leaves, along stems, inside the leaf itself, and on the flowers. Is it hovering over specific plants or crawling along the ground? Is it in the ground?
- Can I see an insect that could be causing the damage? Remember, a bug so tiny that it can't be seen can't chew large holes in leaves. How big can the stomach of an invisible bug be?
- Can I see signs that an insect has been there? This could be aphid skins, frass (a mixture of sawdust and feces left over from boring insects), or the silvery trails left behind by slugs.
- Has anything else happened recently that could account for the damage, such as hail, strong wind, frost, or a heat wave?
- Could anything have been sprayed on a plant or tree, either deliberately

(e.g., fertilizer, insecticide, or soap) or accidentally (e.g., weed killer)?

- Have the leaves been exposed to sudden temperature changes (e.g., sprayed with ice cold water on a hot day)?
- Is there any pattern to the damage, for example, does it affect only certain plants in a bed, one side of a tree, the needles close to a tree trunk, the top branches or stems? If just one side of a tree or plant is damaged, what lies beyond the plant or tree on that side?
- How old is the plant or tree? Has it been planted recently or is it well established? Was it properly planted? Has anything been done near its roots that might affect it (e.g., building a patio, installing an underground sprinkling system, painting a fence, adding more soil to make a flower bed)?
- What other creatures besides bugs could cause the problem—squirrels, rabbits, ground squirrels, birds? You may not think that robins eat flowers or sparrows eat peas, but they do.

Compile as much information as you can, and if you still think there is a problem that requires treatment, either ask a reputable "bug person" to help you identify the problem or do some research in a book or on the Internet. Finding the answer will be much easier now. Happy hunting.

The Symptoms

DAMAGED LEAVES

Although you appreciate the beauty of garden foliage, a tree cares only for survival. As long as it has plenty of leaf surface for photosynthesis, it will be fine with less-than-perfect leaves. Most of us accept, indeed expect, bruises and blemishes on ourselves and so should extend the same tolerance to our trees. Remember, trees did very well on their own, before people had the time and the money to "fix" them.

Don't immediately label a bug crawling around on your plant as a criminal. Sometimes it simply landed there, with no intention of doing any harm. It may even be a good bug; many insects are predators of other insects on plants. The most easily recognized predators, once you have met them, are lady beetle larvae. They are dark colored with orange or red spots and look like tiny alligators. They eat aphids. Don't kill them!

If you determine that uninvited guests are eating the leaves of your plant and overstaying their welcome, then you must choose your weapon. Direct your attack only towards the intended victim, using the least-toxic method available. For example, if you cannot see or get

Problems Caused by Common Prairie Garden Bugs

Plant Group	Problem	Specific Plant(s)	Possible Cause(s)
deciduous trees and shrubs	leaves partly or completely chewed	cottonwood, aspen, willow	leaf beetles (p. 106), spiny elm caterpillar (p. 112)
		elm	spiny elm caterpillar (p. 112)
		willow, poplar	willow sawfly (p. 122)
		apple, poplar, elm, ash, boxelder (Manitoba maple)	cankerworms (p. 114)
	round holes in leaves	rose	leafcutter bee (p. 169)
	chewed leaves, with silken "tents"	chokecherry, fruit trees	uglynest caterpillars (p. 111)
		deciduous trees	tent caterpillars (p. 115)
		aspen	Bruce spanworm (p. 113)
	blisters on leaves	birch, elm, poplar, lilac	leafminers (pp. 119–120)
		purpleleaf sand cherry, cotoneaster, hawthorn, pear, plum	pear sawfly (pear slug) (p. 122)
	speckles on leaves	ash	ash plant bug (p. 102)
	lump on leaf or leaf petiole	hybrid poplar	poplar petiole gall aphid (p. 96) and other gall aphids
	lump on leaf, red	willow	willow redgall sawfly (p. 121)
	lump on male flower	ash	ash flower gall mite (p. 123)
	lump on twig	hybrid poplars	poplar budgall mite (p. 125)
	leaf curl, branch disfigurement	honeysuckle	honeysuckle aphid (p. 97)
	leaf curl	elm	woolly elm aphid (p. 98)
	leaf curl	aspen, willow, poplar, birch, apple	aspen leaf roller caterpillar (p. 118) and other leaf-rolling caterpillars
	twig loss, sticky secretion	willow	black willow aphid (p. 95)

Plant Group	Problem	Specific Plant(s)	Possible Cause(s)
	leaf and twig loss	deciduous trees, shrubs	scales (pp. 99–101)
	branch death	birch	bronze birch borer (p. 103)
	bud drop	roses	rose curculio (p. 109), tarnished plant bug or other lygus bugs (p. 157)
	holes, oozing sap, branch death	aspen, cottonwood, balsam poplar	poplar borer (p. 105)
	holes, cavities	rotting wood	carpenter ants (p. 141)
	branch death	ash	western ash bark beetle (p. 107)
	branch death	elm	elm bark beetles (p. 108)
	branch death, holes, tunnels	hybrid poplars	carpenterworm (p. 110)
conifers	needle deformity, needle loss, white raised teardrop-shaped bumps on needles, branch death	pine, spruce	pine needle scale (p. 86)
	needle loss	spruce	yellow-headed spruce sawfly (p. 91), spruce budworm (p. 90)
	needle loss with silken clusters, mass of frass	spruce, pine	webspinning sawfly (p. 92)
	needle loss, browning	spruce, juniper, Douglas fir	spruce spider mite (p. 93)
	holes and oozing sap at top of tree	spruce, pine	white pine weevil (p. 88)
	deformed leader (top)	spruce, pine	white pine weevil (p. 88)
	swollen pink, purple, or brown branch tips	spruce	spruce gall adelgid (p. 87)
garden plants	holes in leaves	many, close to ground	slug (p. 149)
	plants cut off at base	many	cutworms (pp. 138–139)

Plant Group	Problem	Specific Plant(s)	Possible Cause(s)
	wilting	many	tarnished plant bug or other lygus bugs (p. 157), aphids (p. 158)
	bud drop	many	tarnished plant bug or other lygus bugs (p. 157)
	deformation of growing tip	many	tarnished plant bug or other lygus bugs (p. 157)
	leaf mottling	many	stink bug (p. 157), thrips (p. 161)
	leaf mottling	Virginia creeper, hops	Virginia creeper leafhopper (p. 160)
	terminal bud leaves tied, black debris	delphinium, larkspur, monkshood	delphinium leaftier (p. 167)
	leaf curl	many	various leaf-rolling caterpillars
fruit	red raised blotch on leaf	currant	currant aphid (p. 126)
	chewed leaves	currant	imported currantworm (p. 131)
	deformed fruit	chokecherry	chokecherry midge (p. 128)
	wilted, deformed plants	strawberry	strawberry root weevil (p. 129)
	wormy fruit	currant	currant fruit fly (p. 127)
	wilted leaves, broken canes	raspberry	raspberry crown borer (p. 130)
vegetables	holes in leaves	potato	tuber flea beetle (p. 173), Colorado potato beetle (p. 176)
	tunnels in carrots	carrots	carrot rust fly (p. 174)
	dying	onions	onion root maggot (p. 175)
	holes in leaves	cruciferous vegetables	imported cabbageworm (p. 177), diamondback moth caterpillar (p. 178)
	plants cut off at base	many	cutworms (p. 138)
lawns	dead patches	turf grass	June bug (p. 133), crane fly (p. 58)
	dead patches, white webbing underground, frass	turf grass	sod webworm (p. 137)

Round holes in leaves, especially of roses, may be caused by leafcutter bees (p. 169).

Jagged holes in leaves may be caused by a number of different bugs
(e.g., imported cabbageworm, slug).

Boreholes in a braceletlike pattern are caused by the western ash bark beetle
(*Hylesinus californicus*) (p. 107).

Mined leaves may be caused by a number of different insects, usually called leafminers (pp. 119–120).

Many caterpillars roll leaves for protection (p. 118).

Onion damage is often caused by the onion root maggot
(*Hylemya antiqua*, syn. *Delia antiqua*) (p. 175).

at the targeted bug, contact insecticides are inappropriate. Perhaps caterpillars have made holes in leaves and then rolled up in them to pupate. You can't kill them with sprays when they are rolled up in these sleeping bags, because the spray won't touch their bodies. Or, maybe the culprit has fled. Once pupae become moths and leave, it is useless to worry—you can't kill something that isn't there.

Many fungi cause holes in the leaves of trees and shrubs. In the spring, round, brown fungal spots often appear on leaves when the air is cool and damp. As the weather warms up, the brown spots dry and fall out. Of course, spring is also when gardeners are prowling in their gardens, looking for new growth and potential problems. Just remember, a brown spot with a yellow halo is a sign that a fungus is attacking the leaves, and an insecticide will have no effect on a fungus. In any case, once you have holes in foliage, nothing you spray will make the holes go away. Ignore them.

Heavy winds can cause tears in leaves. If the torn leaves are easily rearranged, like a puzzle, back to their original shape, there are likely no bugs involved. Hail can also do more damage to foliage than most insects ever do. If you return from holidays and find holes and tatters everywhere, don't blame bugs.

The Ant and the Peony

Ants on peonies are a common source of worry. Many people think they are necessary for flower buds to open, and others think that they stop the buds from opening. Neither is true. Some ants are irresistibly drawn to the sweet, sticky substance that coats some peony buds. One theory is that the peony gains some protection against insects that may damage the buds by "offering" the sweet substance to the ants in exchange for the ants "guarding" the buds.

LEAF OR NEEDLE LOSS

Only a few evildoers in the insect world cause significant leaf loss. Tent caterpillars or imported currantworms can strip a deciduous plant rapidly, but they are fairly obvious. If you cannot spot a culprit, and the bark and branches of the tree seem otherwise healthy, then your problem lies elsewhere. Incorrect watering or other cultural problems should be investigated.

Needle loss on conifers should be looked at closely. Needle loss on the inside of conifers is normal and not cause for alarm. However, there are a few small but nasty critters that can cause needle loss (see pp. 103–105). You should be concerned if the loss occurs on new growth or at branch ends.

DAMAGE TO TREE TRUNK OR BRANCHES

There is a small league of tiny creatures that can bore their way into your trees (see pp. 103–105, 107–109). Healthy trees can stand some use of their trunks as "bug condos," but some bugs take their urban development to extremes, given the chance. In these cases it is prudent to intervene on your tree's behalf. Boreholes, piles of sawdust or frass, or oozing sap, especially if accompanied by premature leaf or branch loss, should be investigated and dealt with.

Aphids or scale may cause leaf or twig loss in extreme cases. Check twigs carefully for signs of these nuisances; their presence is often accompanied by a sticky substance, which they excrete. This sticky mess, which may blacken as it gets moldy, can be an annoyance to homeowners. However, mature trees can easily withstand some leaf and twig loss.

Bacteria and fungi are often far more serious problems for trees than insects are. Bacteria are contagious and may cause a tree to die if not dealt with early. Although insects are not the culprits, they may help spread bacteria. Poor pruning practices may also encourage or spread disease.

Fireblight (*Erwinia amylovora*) is a bacterium that attacks trees in the rose family, such as pear, mountain ash, crabapple, and apple. Blackened twigs and blossoms are early signs of fireblight. Trees may show cracked, oozing bark in advanced stages. There is no effective spray for killing this bacterium. Insecticides have no effect at all, because insects don't cause the problem.

Dutch elm disease (DED) is a serious problem for elm trees. It is caused by a fungus (*Ophiostoma ulmi*), which is spread by elm bark beetles. Sudden leaf wilting and subsequent leaf loss are the first signs of DED; then branches die, and eventually the whole tree dies.

Prudent Pruning

Pruning may be done either to improve the appearance of a healthy tree or shrub or to remove weakened or diseased branches. Branches that have been invaded by wood-boring insects can become weakened and break easily in strong wind or under the weight of heavy snow. Weakened branches should be removed, back to healthy wood. There are a few aspects to consider when pruning:

- Make a proper cut. Twigs and small branches can be snipped at a slight angle just beyond a healthy growth point, such as a bud or side branch. Have large branches removed by a good arborist if you are not familiar with the proper technique. Branches should not be cut off flush with the trunk. Make the cut upwards, starting from the bottom of the branch to be removed. Start the cut slightly out from the trunk so as to leave the slight swelling at the base of the branch (called the branch collar), then angle the cut upwards towards the crotch where the branch and trunk meet. If the branch is very heavy, cut it off in sections, making the last cut on the remaining branch stump as described. Consult a good pruning book to be sure of the technique. A proper pruning cut heals as a donut-shaped callus.

- Keep pruning tools sharp. Use the tool (saw, secateur, lopper) appropriate for the task.

- Keep tools clean. If you are pruning a diseased tree or shrub, dip the pruning shears in a solution of one part bleach to ten parts water between each cut to avoid spreading disease from branch to branch.

- Don't use pruning paint or spray on pruning wounds. It creates an impervious coating that provides fungus and bacteria with a safe, sheltered place to grow. Trees survived pruning, wind damage, hail, and the like, for a long time before either product was invented. Trees will callus over just fine by themselves.

- Remove badly diseased trees and shrubs. A diseased tree may host insects that carry bacteria or viruses and spread them to other trees in the neighborhood. A rose with a virus can live for quite some time, but will gradually weaken and die. If the rose is unlikely to survive, it is best to remove it. It is easier to control the spread of disease by removing diseased plants than by trying to find and kill the insects responsible for spreading the problem.

White pine weevil (*Pissodes strobi*) causes the leaders of pine and spruce to curl over in a "shepherd's crook" (p. 88).

Honeysuckle aphid (*Hyadaphis tataricae*) feeding causes unsightly "witches' broom" on honeysuckle (p. 97).

Sometimes weather is the source of tree problems. Sunscald, caused by sunlight in winter, especially reflected off snow, can damage soft-barked trees such as mountain ash and amur chokecherry. The bark warms and swells during a sunny day and then shrinks as it cools down at night. This expansion and contraction can eventually split the bark. The south or southwest side of a trunk is most susceptible since it experiences the greatest range of temperatures. Often these cracks heal completely and cause little harm. Sometimes, however, the cracks serve as an entry point for fungus that grows beneath the bark. Cankers can form as the fungus causes the wood to soften and disintegrate. Branches above the canker, dependent on water moving up the tree, may die. Prune branches affected by fungal cankers back to healthy wood.

DEFORMITIES
Some insects cause stunting or deformed growth on plants. The tarnished plant bug, a type of lygus bug (see p. 157), is a prime example. Substances in their saliva deform fruit, leaves, and growing tips; buds may also not develop properly. Leaders of conifers may be deformed into "shepherd's crooks" by the presence of white pine weevils (see p. 88). Grotesque "witches brooms" may infest honeysuckle as the result of aphids feeding on the plant (see p. 97).

Viruses can be responsible for various deformities, yellow streaks, or odd patterns on leaves, but there are no effective ways to control them. Plants gradually become less healthy, produce fewer blossoms, and grow more slowly, often taking a long time to die. Insects such as aphids can spread viruses, so a plant with a virus is best removed from the garden and thrown in the garbage, not the compost pile. You are not going to win when it comes to aphids—every aphid is born pregnant and able to give birth to more pregnant aphids as soon as it's born—so relax and let the lady beetles feast on them. Spraying with an insecticide won't eliminate enough aphids for virus control, and it will kill lady beetles and other beneficial bugs.

GALLS
Galls are intriguing-looking growths that sometimes form on stems or leaves of plants, trees, and shrubs (see p. 44–45). Although they may resemble cones or berries, they are, in fact, a deformity caused in response to an insect imbedding itself inside the plant to feed or lay eggs. Gall-making insects are often aphids, psyllids, midges, or certain wasps. These insects often choose a specific target plant and create their own distinctive gall, usually remaining in the gall until

they are adults. The gall protects the plant from further trauma and also protects the insect from predation. It does no good to spray insecticides on galls, but it does help to know that galls are seldom a problem for the plant. Branches with galls can be removed if desired.

Common Name Conundrums

Although scientific names are long and hard to pronounce, common names can be just as perplexing. One person's Junebug is another person's May beetle. Common names vary from region to region, and sometimes it is hard to get consensus about which bugs we are referring to, or what type of bug it might be.

Although we know that a woolly bear isn't a bear, what about a Junebug? Is it a real bug? Is a caddisfly some type of fly? A simple rule for making some sense of common names lies in the way the ending descriptor, such as fly or bug is used. The convention (although not universally used) is that real flies belonging to the order Diptera always have the ending fly as a separate word, such as hover fly or crane fly. Caddisflies have the 'fly' included in one word, so it isn't a real fly, and is in fact it's own order, the Trichoptera. Stink bugs are 'real' bugs in the order Hemiptera, and Junebugs are actually a type of beetle.

"Wining" About Bugs

In the last century, a homopteran called the grape phylloxera nearly destroyed the grapevines of France. This North American aphid relative forms galls on the roots of grapevines. North American labruscan grapevines are resistant to the pylloxera, but not so the European grapevines. When it was accidentally introduced to Europe, an American named Riley saved French viticulture by grafting the European vines onto hardy North American rootstock. So today the fine wines of France owe their continued viability to a lowly North American grapevine.

Common Galls Found on Prairie Trees and Shrubs

Spruce gall adelgid (*Adelges cooleyi*) (p. 87)

Poplar petiole gall aphid (*Pemphigus bursarius*) (p. 96)

Willow redgall sawfly (*Pontania proxima*) (p. 121)

Poplar budgall mite (*Eriophyes parapopuli*) (p. 125)

Eriophyid gall mite (*Eriophyes* spp.) (p. 123)

Currant aphid (*Cryptomyzus ribis*) (p. 126)

Chokecherry midge (*Contarinia virginianiae*) (p. 128)

6

PANDORA'S BOTTLE: USING PESTICIDES

If you are going to open Pandora's bottle, there are some things you should know. Many insects are good, and many more are neither harmful nor good—they are just "there." Undoubtedly, some insects damage garden plants, invade homes, or irritate pets and people. You may be tempted to use pesticides to kill them and then get on with your gardening. However, you have a responsibility to others, to the neighborhood, and to yourself to spray wisely.

Pesticides should rarely be needed in a garden. It is beyond the scope of this book to recommend specific pesticides to address specific problems. This chapter is intended simply to help you choose and use pesticides sensibly.

The most important step in deciding to spray or not to spray is to identify the culprit. Next, you must decide if action is warranted. Don't assume that plants suffer only one problem at a time. This doesn't happen when raising children, balancing a bank account, or building a house, so it isn't likely to be common in your garden either. For example, if a hole-ridden plant has aphids on it, you might conclude that aphids made the holes. If you did, you would be wrong. Aphids make a sticky mess and suck plant juices. However, a few weeks earlier the damaged plant may have hosted caterpillars, definitely capable of chewing holes in leaves. But it's too late to kill the caterpillars—they've pupated, emerged as adults, and left—and the aphids aren't doing enough damage to worry about. So, instead of worrying, enjoy your garden and accept all its idiosyncrasies, the same way you accept them in your friends.

Not all pesticides are alike. If you decide to use a pesticide, you must first choose the right one. Then, before applying it, acquaint yourself with the pesticide's toxicity and the guidelines for its safe use.

About Pesticides

Before using any kind of pesticide in your garden, it is important to understand the nature of pesticides. A pesticide is a chemical used to kill a pest.

Taking "Cides"

Pesticide - kills anything designated as a pest, either plant or animal

Insecticide - kills insects

Miticide or acaricide - kills mites

Molluscicide - kills slugs and snails

Fungicide - kills fungi

Herbicide - kills plants

All pesticides are chemicals—even those you buy labeled "organic," "botanical," or "natural." Chemicals in pesticides may be relatively non-toxic or highly toxic. They usually kill bugs by interfering with one or more of their bodily functions. Even dormant oil is a chemical, although it does its deadly work by smothering pests rather than by poisoning them.

Pesticides are classified as inorganic, botanical (natural organic), or synthetic organic. Inorganic pesticides include boric acid, copper, arsenic, and Bordeaux Mixture (a blend of copper sulfate and hydrated lime) and were common agricultural controls before the advent of the synthetic chemicals that were developed after World War II. Botanical chemicals or natural organic pesticides such as rotenone and pyrethrum are extracted from plants. Synthetic organic pesticides such as diazinon and malathion are devised by man. Many synthetic compounds are taken off the market as the negative consequences of their long-term use become known. New chemicals deemed safer might take their place.

To select a pesticide that is right for the job, ask yourself the following questions:

- Is the pesticide registered for the bugs and plants I want to target? Always use the right control, not just whatever is handy. Some pesticides can damage certain plants.

- Is it toxic to people, pets, or birds? Many pesticides that are relatively non-toxic to warm-blooded animals may be exceedingly toxic to fish. If you have a pond, be very careful not to let pesticides drift into the water.

- Is it toxic to other insects and spiders? Don't kill the "good guys."

- How mobile is it? Will it move through soil or groundwater?

- How long will it remain toxic after I apply it? Will it break down to harmless components?

- How effective will it be on my target pest? Don't introduce chemicals into the environment if they are not going to do a good job.

What's on a Label?

The label on a pesticide package contains a great deal of useful information, but it is rarely read. The printing is small and most people assume they won't understand it anyway. What can you learn from a label?

- The trade name (can be different for the same ingredients from different companies)
- The category, which indicates who may use it (only those for domestic use are considered here)
- Whether it is ready to use, must be dissolved in water, or is a wettable powder
- Hazard symbols (for poison, flammable, explosive, or corrosive)
- Pest Control Product (PCP) Registration Number, which indicates it has met all requirements and is registered in Canada; Environmental Protection Agency (EPA) Registration Number in the United States.
- Guarantee of active ingredient
- Manufacturer's name and address (necessary in the event of accidental poisoning)
- What pests it is legally registered to control
- What plants it is legally registered to be used on
- What temperature range it is most effective in
- How often to apply it
- What can be harmed by the spray (e.g., flowers on the plant, fish in a pond or aquarium)
- How to store it and for how long
- First aid in case of poisoning (symptoms, antidote for physician's use)
- First aid for accidents on skin or in eyes
- Days to harvest (the number of days before fruits and vegetables can be safely eaten after spraying)

- How much does it cost? Is it cheaper to replace a sick four-dollar plant than it is to buy a twenty-dollar pesticide?
- What is its shelf life? Avoid using pesticides that have been stored for more than a couple of years. They may no longer be effective, though not necessarily less toxic. Do not throw old chemicals in the garbage.

Contact your local sanitation service for proper disposal sites.

- Is it still legal? Old chemicals you've stored in the garage may have been taken off the market, or they may not be legal where you want to use them (near waterways, for example). Don't use these chemicals. Their use has been restricted or prohibited for a reason. Knowledgable staff in stores where pesticides are sold should be able to tell you if a pesticide is still registered for home use.

Read the Label, Read the Label, and Read the Label

To be a responsible pesticide user, you must be informed and confident about your choice of pesticide. It helps to consult with staff at a reputable garden center who are knowledgeable about insecticides and who have pesticide dispenser certificates. It also helps to read the whole label on a pesticide container, including all the fine print.

An insecticide must be registered for *both the targeted bug and the plant* before you can be sure it is safe and effective. This information is written on the label. Some insecticides can seriously harm certain plants, but have no negative effects on others.

Do *not* change the recommended concentration of a pesticide, in order to make it work better or faster. The manufacturers want you to be happy with their product and have gone to considerable effort to provide a product that is effective for the problem it is registered for, if used as instructed. If it does what it is supposed to do, you will continue to use products from that company. By reading, and obeying, the label, you are most likely to be satisfied with the results.

Contact vs. Systemic Insecticides

Most insecticides sold today kill pests on contact only. The insecticide must hit the bugs to kill them, so spraying before the bugs arrive or after they have left has little or no effect. Some contact pesticides will kill insects that come in contact with leaves that have been sprayed, but this process is usually fairly short-lived. Many modern contact insecticides are reasonably safe for humans and pets, some more so than others.

Insecticidal soaps are soap-based contact pesticides. Although they are non-toxic to people and mammals, they are not, as is commonly thought, chemical-free. They kill soft-bodied insects on contact only and must be rinsed off the plant soon after spraying. Plants do not like their leaves coated with sticky material.

Chemical Classification of Pesticides

Chemical Category	Synthetic Family	Examples (generic names)	Comment
inorganic		boric acid, copper, sulfur, diatomaceous earth	many are ancient remedies
botanical (natural organic)		garlic, limonene, neem, nicotine, pyrethrum, rotenone	some, like rotenone, are toxic; tend to break down rapidly
synthetic organics	carbamate	carbaryl	break down rapidly; also detrimental to useful pollinators
	chlorinated hydrocarbon	chlordane, DDT	toxic and persistent; many, like chlordane, have been or will be removed from the market; dispose of such chemicals properly
	organo-phosphate	diazinon, malathion, dimethoate, chlorpyrifos	break down relatively rapidly compared to chlorinated hydrocarbons; malathion is much safer than diazinon; dimethoate is a systemic pesticide
	pyrethroid	permethrin	synthetic pyrethrin is designed to be safer for mammals than natural pyrethrin
	horticultural oil	dormant oil	acts by suffocating organisms; may "suffocate" leaves also, so use on woody plants when they are dormant (leafless)
	insecticidal soap	insecticidal soap	acts by dissolving the waxy coating on a bug's exoskeleton, exposing it to dehydration; rinse off foliage after use
	insect growth regulator (IGR)	may be available to home gardeners in the future	the newest "third generation" pesticides; interfere with an insect's growth cycle; non-toxic to vertebrates

Systemic pesticides move within the plant sap and make leaves poisonous to insects that chew on them. Systemics can also be absorbed through human skin and can be quite toxic to people. They are not appropriate for spraying. Some must be watered into soil. Read the label!

Formulations

Pesticides come in liquids, wettable powders, and dusts. Liquids are sold ready-to-use in spray bottles or as concentrates. Concentrates are less expensive in the long run, but are not practical if you only need a small amount and would need to store it for years before you use all of it. Concentrates are usually applied with a sprayer on the end of a garden hose. Put the liquid into the container and set to the recommended concentration, using the dial on the sprayer. Containers used for pesticides should be kept only for that purpose and labeled accordingly.

Better Living through Chemistry?

The new synthetic pesticides that arrived on the market after World War II seemed like a dream come true. The offerings of science and technology promised to make our lives better. Disease-carrying insects would no longer bother people and livestock, and our fruits and vegetables would grow ripe and plump without being full of holes or half-eaten. Yet, although pesticides have made some important contributions to our quality of life, there are many cases of pesticide use backfiring. Consider the following well-documented examples:

- Houseflies became resistant to DDT in 1947, only two years after this chemical was introduced to control them. Insects reproduce rapidly, and all it took was a few individual flies resistant to DDT to generate a new breed of "superflies."

- Insecticides used to control codling moth larvae in apple orchards (those of "wormy apple" fame) eliminated the moth, but also eliminated the natural enemies of a certain red-banded leaf roller. This leaf roller has thrived in a world devoid of its predators and has become an agricultural pest in its own right.

These examples, in addition to the obvious danger of toxicity to people, pets, wild animals, and birds, reinforce the reality that pesticides are not a panacea. They are only one tool for pest control, and one that should not be used lightly.

Wettable powders must be added to water in a container, such as a watering can or pump-type hand sprayer, and be shaken periodically to keep the particles dissolved. A hose-end sprayer isn't practical to use with wettable powders, as sprayers only measure liquids in milliliters per liter.

A dust can be sprinkled directly onto leaves or flower buds. Insects will retain some on their bodies as they come in contact with the dust. Some dusts are more poisonous than others; be careful you don't inhale the dust while applying it.

Classification of Pesticides

These days, some older toxic pesticides are being removed from the market, while newer, safer ones are being introduced. Pesticides sold to gardeners generally have three levels of names: a brand name, a generic name (e.g., malathion), and a chemical name (long and hard to understand).

Safety

When working with garden pesticides, safety comes first. You must consider your own safety, and that of your family, pets, neighbors, wild birds, and other creatures. Let your neighbors know when and what you are spraying if you are treating a large area or using something toxic to people and pets.

You also need to consider the safety of the plants you are trying to protect. Pesticides used inappropriately might injure plants more than the pest you have decided to wage war against.

A Word about "Organic"

Organic: The word "organic" sounds safe and good, and organic gardening is a laudable goal. However, organic compounds are simply those that are carbon-based; DDT is an organic compound. All organic compounds, whether naturally derived or synthetic, have their own characteristic toxicity and persistence.

Botanical: That sounds better, or does it? Botanical compounds are naturally occurring, organic substances. Some botanical pesticides are relatively safe, and others, like nicotine, are highly toxic. Many famous poisons, such as belladonna and digitalis, come straight from Mother Nature.

DRESS APPROPRIATELY

Get into the habit of wearing rubber, not cloth, gloves when handling pesticides and rubber boots or shoes that can be rinsed off with a hose. If you are spraying a tree, wear a wide-brimmed hat. Don't wear a mask when using sprays that are available to the home gardener. A paper mask filters dusts, but is dangerous to use with liquids as it collects the moist insecticide right in front of your nose. If a chemical is so toxic that a respirator is required, it is too toxic for home use.

USE GOOD TECHNIQUE

Don't spray into the wind so that the chemical blows into your face, and don't look up into a tree as you are spraying it from directly below. Spray up at an angle from a distance so the spray doesn't fall onto your face. Keep children and pets out of the garden until the toxic effect has dissipated. Common sense? Yes, but it seems to be not quite as common as it used to be.

Consider hanging noisemakers such as chimes in a sprayed tree to frighten off birds. Small bushes can be covered with breathable fabric or mesh to keep birds off. Most insecticides will damage flowers, so if there are flowers nearby, cover them before spraying. Covering blossoms might also save useful pollinating insects from ruin.

CHECK THE WEATHER

Consider the outside conditions before spraying. Do not spray on a windy day, for obvious reasons. If possible, spray in the morning, when it is cool. If you spray under a hot sun, the water in which the chemical is dissolved will evaporate quickly and leave the concentrated chemical to bake on the leaves. Only a light spray is necessary; there is no point in having liquid drip off the tree onto the ground.

DAYS TO HARVEST

All insecticides registered for use on edible food have a "days to harvest" indication on the label—the number of days between spraying the plant and eating it that is deemed safe. These pesticides have been rigorously tested to assure you that eating plant leaves, fruit, or vegetables after they have been sprayed is safe if you follow the directions.

Many worrisome concerns surround the use of pesticides, and they will change constantly for years to come. New and safer products are being developed, such as a non-poisonous slug bait, to replace the very toxic ones previously in use. But can we also learn to accept less than perfect gardens? Modifying our expectations and adopting more of a "live and let live" attitude seem a small price to pay to achieve a less-toxic world.

Bug Profiles

7

THE AERIALISTS

You can observe the insects described in this section buzzing or flitting through your garden. These insects are likely to be pollinators of flowers or predators of other insects. Although all flying insects are adults, their juvenile stages might also be doing nice or not-so-nice things amongst your garden plants. If this is the case, these juveniles are described in other chapters.

Many of the insects in this section are described at the family level. It is far beyond the scope of this book to list the dozens of species in each family that might visit your garden.

In the case of butterflies and moths, a typical example from each family that might be found on the prairies is presented. If you are a butterfly and moth enthusiast, you'll want to arm yourself with a good guide for your area and consult some of the excellent books on butterfly or wildlife gardening that are available. Notable caterpillars are described in other chapters.

Of the two groups of lepidopterans, moths and butterflies, moths are the least loved. People are less familiar with the diversity and beauty of moths because they are mainly nocturnal and most are not brightly colored. Although a number of moth larvae are classified as pests and can, in some cases, do quite a bit of damage to gardens or crops, these truly are the exceptions. This chapter includes a very small number of the moths that will enchant a gardener.

Dragonflies and Damselflies

Order Odonata
Families Coenagrionidae, Lestidae (damselflies)
Families Aeshnidae, Libellulidae (dragonflies)

BUG AT A GLANCE

TYPE OF BUG: damselflies, dragonflies

SIZE: 20 to 110 mm (¾ to 4⅓ in.) long

WHAT THEY LOOK LIKE: both have narrow, tapered bodies and four narrow wings; dragonflies hold their wings open at right angles to the body, whereas most damselflies hold their wings closed at an angle above their body

WHERE YOU FIND THEM: usually near water

WHEN YOU FIND THEM: spring to fall, depending on the species

WHAT THEY EAT: both nymphs and adults eat a variety of insects

FRIEND OR FOE: always a friend, and handsome too

WHAT TO DO: marvel at these agile hunters

BUG BIO

Dragonflies and damselflies, together called odonates, have been on this earth since Carboniferous times (360–285 million years ago). They proceed through gradual metamorphosis, but unlike many families of insects that undergo gradual metamorphosis, the adult is profoundly different from the nymph. In fact, the nymph is aquatic, and the adult is a creature of the sky. The nymphal stage may last from as little as a few months to several years, depending on the species. A nymph typically proceeds through eight to fifteen instars.

Aquatic dragonfly nymphs are somewhat cylindrical or flattened; the breathing gills are contained within the rectum. Damselfly nymphs tend to be slender and have three characteristic featherlike gills at the hind end. Voracious predators, these nymphs consume aquatic arthropods, tadpoles, and even small fish that venture near. They have a special "flip-lip" lower jaw that can be sprung rapidly to catch prey while the nymph remains otherwise stationary.

The final instar emerges from the water onto a reed or some other suitable surface and breaks out of its casing to reveal the slender-bodied and gauzy-winged adult. Over a period of several minutes, blood is pumped through the body and wings to expand and harden them. During this time the new adult is very vulnerable.

Adults live only a few months and all their energy is directed towards eating and mating (wouldn't you like to be reincarnated as a dragonfly?). The actual mating of odonates is a remarkable feat, unique in nature. The male's genital opening is at the hind end, as in most other arthropods, but he must transfer his sperm to a secondary organ right behind the legs. Having done this, the male finds a female and grabs her by the head or by the neck. Both adults then curve their abdomens around until the female's genital opening is joined with the male's secondary organ, in an arrangement called the "wheel position." If that isn't strange enough, they do this while flying.

The female usually skims low over water to deposit her eggs. Males may accompany the females while they lay their eggs, sometimes still gripped to the female's head. Once her eggs are laid, the female may return several times to areas where males patrol, for successive matings and egg-layings.

Dragonflies and damselflies hunt by sight and have some of the best eyesight of all insects. They catch flying insects between their legs and take them to a roosting site to be eaten.

Damselfly Myths and Legends

It's not surprising that these distinctive insects have become endowed with mystical powers over the ages. Damselflies were regarded suspiciously in old England as "devil's darning needles." It was said that if you went to sleep by a stream on a summer's day, damselflies would use their long, thin bodies to sew your eyelids shut. A useful variation of this tale was that bad children could have their mouths sewn shut.

Crane fly

Family Tipulidae

BUG AT A GLANCE (illustration p. 61)
> **TYPE OF BUG:** fly
> **SIZE:** 12 to 24 mm (½ to 1 in.) long
> **WHAT IT LOOKS LIKE:** resembles a giant mosquito; larva is an elongated cylindrical grub
> **WHERE YOU FIND IT:** adult might be found flying clumsily around windows at night; larva is found in soil, water, or under turf grass, depending on the species
> **WHEN YOU FIND IT:** summer
> **WHAT IT EATS:** adult may not eat; larva eats decaying vegetable matter, or in the case of the introduced European crane fly *(Tipula palidosa)*, turf grass roots
> **FRIEND OR FOE:** benign
> **WHAT TO DO:** there are no pest species on the prairies

BUG BIO

Like all flies, the crane fly undergoes complete metamorphosis. The larvae, known as leatherjackets, overwinter in soil or water, or under the lawn, depending on the species. Pupation occurs in summer. Adults only live a few days to mate, and normally do not eat. Eggs are laid on soil or in water.

Although there are over fifteen hundred species of crane flies in North America, it is the introduced species *(Tipula palidosa)* that has earned infamy as a turf grass pest. This species has not yet been reported as a pest species on the prairies. Other crane fly species are benign and likely beneficial, since the larvae consume decomposing vegetation.

Robber fly

Family Asilidae

BUG AT A GLANCE (illustration p. 61)
> **TYPE OF BUG:** predaceous fly
> **SIZE:** usually 8 to 14 mm (⅓ to ⅝ in.) long
> **WHAT IT LOOKS LIKE:** waspish-looking, hairy, slim-bodied fly with

long legs; flattened, wormlike larva lives in soil and is unlikely to be seen

WHERE YOU FIND IT: on branch tips near open spaces, watching for unwary insects flying by

WHEN YOU FIND IT: spring to fall, depending on the species

WHAT IT EATS: adult eats other flying insects; larva eats vegetable matter and other insect larvae encountered in the soil

FRIEND OR FOE: friend, although it may eat other friendly insects

WHAT TO DO: take a few minutes to observe it making its hunting sorties

BUG BIO

Eggs are laid just under the soil surface. Larvae creep through the soil or leaf litter, eating vegetable matter and any insect larvae they happen to come across. The larvae overwinter in the soil. In summer, the pupae wiggle to the surface when they are ready to transform into adults.

Robber flies are the flycatchers of the insect world, and their behavior is easily compared to those birds. The adult fly perches on the end of a twig where it has a clear view and flies out periodically to investigate objects that come close. If the object is a prey item, it may be intercepted in midair and seized with the fly's long legs. The prey is brought back to the perch, where the robber fly sucks the juices of the hapless prey. Courtship displays by the male to the female are important, since the male does not want to be mistaken for a meal. About nine hundred recognized robber fly species exist in North America.

Hover fly

Family Syrphidae

BUG AT A GLANCE

TYPE OF BUG: predaceous fly

SIZE: from 2 to 40 mm ($\frac{1}{10}$ to $1\frac{1}{2}$ in.) long

WHAT IT LOOKS LIKE: fly is black, blue, metallic, striped, or spotted; larva is sluglike and tapered at one end

WHERE YOU FIND IT: adult is found wherever there are flowers; larva lives amongst prey such as aphids

WHEN YOU FIND IT: spring to fall, depending on the species

WHAT IT EATS: adult feeds on nectar and pollen; larvae of most species are carnivorous, consuming vast quantities of insects such as aphids, thrips, and small caterpillars

FRIEND OR FOE: friend; love them because they are pollinators, love their babies because they munch aphids

WHAT TO DO: put that can of bug spray away and admire your garden

BUG BIO

Female hover flies lay their eggs near aphids, or in decaying flesh or dung: in other words, wherever there is a suitable food supply for the young. Upon hatching, the hungry larvae begin digging into this thoughtfully provided bounty, eating vast quantities of aphids and other insects. Larvae burrow in soil to overwinter. The following summer, the larvae pupate and emerge as adults. Males are thought to establish a route and patrol energetically for females.

Many species disguise themselves as bees or wasps, but their amazing hovering ability and the fact that they have only two wings and very short antennae identify them as hover flies.

Take time to become familiar with these very desirable flies, as you will enjoy your flowers even more, instead of retreating to the house for fear of being stung. Although these flies are common, and next to bees, extremely important pollinators, little is known about the nearly nine hundred species of hover fly identified in North America.

Hover fly (Family Syrphidae)

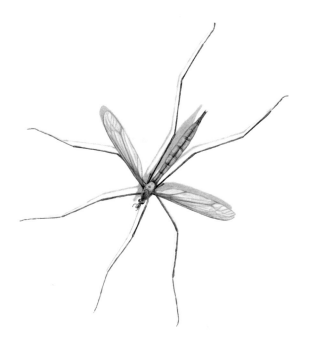

Crane fly (Family Tipulidae) (p. 58)

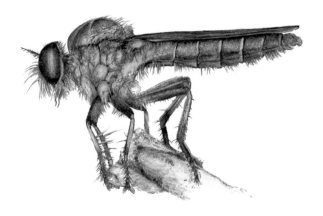

Robber fly (Family Asilidae) (p. 58)

Tachinid fly

Family Tachinidae

BUG AT A GLANCE (illustration p. 64)

TYPE OF BUG: parasitoid fly

SIZE: 5 to 15 mm (⅕ to ⅜ in.) long

WHAT IT LOOKS LIKE: a hairy housefly, brown to black or reddish

WHERE YOU FIND IT: everywhere

WHEN YOU FIND IT: spring to fall, depending on the species

WHAT IT EATS: adult eats honeydew; larva eats its host from the inside out

FRIEND OR FOE: friend; a very common and effective but underappreciated ally

WHAT TO DO: nothing; isn't it time to weed?

BUG BIO

The female lays her eggs on the back of a host insect, often just behind the head, where the unlucky host will have a hard time dislodging it. After hatching, the larvae burrow into their host where they feed, eventually killing it. The fly may pupate within the pupa of the host, or it may exit the dead insect to pupate elsewhere.

Although the life cycle of this family may seem to be the stuff of science fiction, it is part of the natural process that goes on in your garden all the time, very often to your benefit.

There are nearly thirteen hundred recognized species of this family in North America, and little is known about most of them. Some may be used deliberately as biological controls.

Caddisfly

Order Trichoptera
Family Hydroptilidae (micro-caddisfly)
Family Limnephilidae (northern caddisfly)
Family Phryganeidae (large caddisfly)

BUG AT A GLANCE (illustration p. 64)

TYPE OF BUG: caddisfly
SIZE: up to 20 mm (¾ in.) long; micro-caddisfly, 3 to 6 mm (⅛ to ¼ in.) long
WHAT IT LOOKS LIKE: adult is often mistaken for a small moth or fly; it is long-legged, with long antennae
WHERE YOU FIND IT: widely distributed near lakes, ponds, and streams
WHEN YOU FIND IT: adults swarm for 2 to 6 weeks in summer, usually in 5 to 7 year cycles
WHAT IT EATS: larva is carnivorous, herbivorous, or omnivorous, depending on the species; adult of most species does not feed
FRIEND OR FOE: benign
WHAT TO DO: nothing

BUG BIO

Caddisflies undergo complete metamorphosis. Eggs are laid on water or on marginal vegetation. The aquatic nymphs can live for many years before emerging as adults. The nymphs of many species create a case around themselves out of bits of aquatic vegetation or other debris for protection and camouflage. Pupation takes place in a sac or case. The adults emerge from the pupal case at the water's surface and only live for a short time, dying soon after mating and laying eggs.

Most people, except those who engage in fly-fishing, are not very familiar with caddisflies. Gardeners who live near bodies of water will discover them when they emerge en masse in the spring to mate. These completely harmless insects will not chew on your plants or on you either, for that matter. The adult's job is only to mate and lay eggs; most adults do not eat at all, and once their mission is complete, they die.

Although swarming caddisflies may interupt your summer barbecue plans, remember that it is not safe or legal to spray toxins near a waterway. Caddisfly larvae are a major food source for many fish, including trout, and the adults are a boon to birds that are returning from an arduous migration. So, instead of bemoaning the swarm, get out the binoculars to scout for all of the insect-eating birds that are enjoying this bonanza.

Tachinid fly (Family Tachinidae) (p. 62)

Caddisfly (Order Trichoptera) (p. 63)

Yellowpatch or Peck's skipper (*Polites coras*, syn. *P. peckius*) (p. 65)

Yellowpatch or Peck's skipper

Family Hesperiidae
Polites coras, syn. *P. peckius*

BUG AT A GLANCE (illustration p. 64)

TYPE OF BUG: butterfly in the skipper family

SIZE: wingspan 20 to 30 mm (¾ to 1¼ in.)

WHAT IT LOOKS LIKE: orange-brown butterfly with a fuzzy body and yellow patches on the wings; caterpillar is dark reddish brown, mottled with light brown, and has lengthwise black stripes

WHERE YOU FIND IT: grassy areas, meadows

WHEN YOU FIND IT: adult is seen in July and August; one generation

WHAT IT EATS: adult drinks nectar, especially from plants of the legume family, and may be attracted to dung or carrion; caterpillar eats grass species

FRIEND OR FOE: benign; useful pollinator

WHAT TO DO: check it off your butterfly "life list"

BUG BIO

Tiny eggs are laid on grasses. The caterpillars that emerge weave daytime shelters of silk and leaves. The caterpillars overwinter within a silken shelter as a chrysalis, usually at the base of a host plant. There may be two generations in the southern part of its range (adults flying in May and June, and again in August and September), and one generation in the north or at high elevations (in July and August). Compared to other butterflies, the yellowpatch skipper is not fussy about its habitat, and thus its range is expanding.

Skippers form a group distinct from other butterflies and have many characteristics that are similar to those of moths, including stout hairy bodies, duller colors, and spinning silk about themselves in their pupal stage. Some groups of skippers hold their fore wings and hind wings at different angles. They are named for their skipping flight.

Three subfamilies of skippers can be found on the prairies: the spread-wing skippers (Pyrginae) that hold their wings out to the side; the skipperlings (Heteropterinae); and the grass skippers (Hesperiinae). Besides the yellowpatch skipper, which is a grass skipper, the silver-spotted skipper (*Epargyreus clarus*) and the common checkered skipper (*Pyrgus communis*), both spread-wing skippers, might visit your prairie garden.

Canadian tiger swallowtail

Family Papilionidae
Papilio canadensis

BUG AT A GLANCE (illustration p. 68)

TYPE OF BUG: butterfly in the swallowtail family

SIZE: wingspan 85 to 100 mm (3⅜ to 4 in.)

WHAT IT LOOKS LIKE: a large, yellow butterfly with black stripes and distinctive hind wing "tails"; caterpillar is large, bright green, and bulbous at the front with two distinct eye-spots, and it has a special yellow or red repellent organ called an osmaterium that it can extend from behind its head

WHERE YOU FIND IT: wherever there are aspens

WHEN YOU FIND IT: adult is seen from May to mid-July; one generation

WHAT IT EATS: adult relishes lilac and dandelion; caterpillar eats aspen leaves, but may also munch on willow or crabapple

FRIEND OR FOE: benign; a useful pollinator

WHAT TO DO: buy a good butterfly guide and fill your garden with things that attract butterflies

BUG BIO

Globular eggs are laid on aspen, willow, or crabapple leaves. The caterpillars that emerge weave silken mats within shelters of curled leaves. The overwintering chrysalis hangs right side up and is slung with a loop of silk. There is one generation, flying from May to mid-July.

This family includes some of the largest, most impressive and downright tropical looking butterflies on the prairies. In fact, most of the butterflies in this family are tropicals. Swallowtails (at least all of those found on the prairies) are distinguished by a pair of tail-like appendages on the hind wings.

Other swallowtails, such as the black swallowtail (*P. polyxenes*), old-world swallowtail (*P. machaon*), and anise swallowtail (*P. zelicaon*), might also be spotted.

Cabbage white butterfly

Family Pieridae
Pieris rapae

BUG AT A GLANCE (illustration p. 68)
TYPE OF BUG: butterfly in the white and sulphur family
SIZE: wingspan 30 to 35 mm (1¼ to 1⅜ in.)
WHAT IT LOOKS LIKE: pale, creamy-colored butterfly; male has a dark spot on each fore wing and female has two spots
WHERE YOU FIND IT: widely distributed
WHEN YOU FIND IT: adult is seen from spring to fall; several generations
WHAT IT EATS: adult sips nectar; caterpillar eats cruciferous vegetables
FRIEND OR FOE: benign; they are not a problem unless you have a nice juicy cabbage or broccoli crop that you want to keep all to yourself
WHAT TO DO: nothing
(see p. 177 for a profile of the caterpillar, the imported cabbageworm)

BUG BIO

The butterflies in this family, among the most common butterflies seen on the prairies, are usually white, yellow, or orange and may have black spots or other dark markings on the wings. Many species in this family have a very narrow range of host plants, typically in the legume and cruciform families. Although most species are fairly plain looking, many have invisible ultraviolet patterns on their wings, used for courtship. The sexes are often colored or patterned differently.

Although rued by vegetable gardeners, the cabbage white gives some cheer, being one of the first butterflies to appear in spring and one of the last to disappear before the onslaught of cold weather.

The yellowish, vase-shaped eggs are laid singly on the host plants. The caterpillars feast on cruciferous vegetables, often penetrating deep within the plant. The speckled chrysalis hangs from a silk button and is slung with a loop of silk. There may be two or three generations a year on the prairies, and more in southern climates. This butterfly normally overwinters as a chrysalis.

The checkered white (*Pontia protodice*) and the orange sulphur (*Colias eurytheme*) are two other members of this family that you might spot in your garden.

Canadian tiger swallowtail (*Papilio canadensis*) (p. 66)

Cabbage white and imported cabbageworm (*Pieris rapae*) (p. 67)

Spring azure

Family Lycaenidae
Celastrina ladon

BUG AT A GLANCE

TYPE OF BUG: butterfly in the copper and blue family

SIZE: wingspan 25 to 30 mm (1 to 1¼ in.)

WHAT IT LOOKS LIKE: small butterfly; top wing of the male is blue; female is less brightly colored with black outlining wing margins; caterpillar is flattened and somewhat sluglike

WHERE YOU FIND IT: anywhere host plants are found

WHEN YOU FIND IT: adult is seen from June to August

WHAT IT EATS: caterpillar often eats flowering parts of dogwoods or cherry trees

FRIEND OR FOE: benign

WHAT TO DO: marvel at its brilliant colors

BUG BIO

The small butterflies in this family are usually blue, brown, or orange, depending on the species. Males are often more brilliantly colored than females. The blue color is due to light reflected from the wing scales and not pigmentation. Male blues can be attracted to suitable mineral puddling sites—mud puddles rich in nutrients. Make a "puddle" in a shallow dish using clay soil, water, and a bit of salt.

The female lays single eggs on the flower buds of a host plant. The rounded chrysalis is formed in ground litter where it overwinters. Spring azures fly from June to August. Caterpillars may secrete sugary substances that are attractive to ants, and these ants provide the caterpillars some protection from other insect predators.

The summer azure (*Celastrina neglecta*) is similar to the spring azure, with whitish markings on the upper wing and pale whitish hind wings dotted with some dark spots. It has one generation per year, flying from June to October.

Another butterfly in this family that may be seen in prairie gardens is the grey hairstreak (*Strymon melinus*), which is one of the most widely dispersed butterflies on the continent because it is not a fussy eater. It is a small, grayish blue butterfly with a small tail on the hind wing that is characteristic of hairstreaks. On the prairies, it favors legumes and mallows.

Mourningcloak butterfly

Family Nymphalidae
Nymphalis antiopa

BUG AT A GLANCE (illustration p. 72)

TYPE OF BUG: butterfly in the brushfoot family
SIZE: wingspan 60 to 80 mm (2½ to 3¼ in.)
WHAT IT LOOKS LIKE: a large butterfly that can be confused with no other; it has purplish brown wings with a bright yellow border on the outer edge of the rear wings and a line of iridescent blue spots inside the yellow border; its distinctive caterpillar is the spiny elm caterpillar
WHERE YOU FIND IT: wherever host plants are found
WHEN YOU FIND IT: adult is seen in early spring, again in June and July, and again in fall
WHAT IT EATS: tree sap, sometimes rotting fruit, occasionally flower nectar
FRIEND OR FOE: friend and foe, depending on your philosophy
WHAT TO DO: it is one of the earliest butterflies seen in spring, so welcome it (see p. 112 for a description of the conspicuous spiny elm caterpillar)

BUG BIO

Adults emerge in early spring from hibernation and lay their eggs in groups encircling the twigs of host plants. Caterpillars feed gregariously in communal webs in elm trees. The tan to gray chrysalis hangs upside down and has a spiny appearance. Adults emerge in June or July to feed briefly, then may go dormant until fall when they feed to store energy for overwintering.

This large family of butterflies includes the fritillaries, admirals, and tortoiseshells. They are called brushfoots because their front feet are shortened and brushlike and are not used for walking. The caterpillars are usually spiny and may have hornlike projections on either end of the body.

Other butterflies in this diverse family that you may encounter in your prairie garden are the variegated fritillary (*Euptoieta claudia*), Milbert's tortoiseshell (*Nymphalis milberti*), gray comma (*Polygonia progne*), red admiral (*Vanessa atalanta*), and painted lady (*V. cardui*).

Monarch butterfly

Family Danaidae
Danaus plexippus

BUG AT A GLANCE (illustration p. 72)

TYPE OF BUG: milkweed butterfly

SIZE: wingspan 90 to 100 mm (3½ to 4 in.)

WHAT IT LOOKS LIKE: adult has dark orange wings with black veins and edge markings, and white spots sprinkled at the hind wing margin; caterpillar is black with yellow-and-white stripes, and a pair of prominent black filaments at both the front and back ends

WHERE YOU FIND IT: wherever host plants are found

WHEN YOU FIND IT: summer, some years

WHAT IT EATS: caterpillar eats milkweeds and dogbanes

FRIEND OR FOE: benign

WHAT TO DO: be amazed and enjoy it

BUG BIO

If any insect were to be considered an ambassador species for insects, the monarch could be it. Its yearly migration north from overwintering grounds in Mexico is an amazing story. In late summer, the monarchs begin migrating to their wintering grounds in the mountains just west of Mexico City. The lucky ones that make it there don't do much except rest and drink occasionally (a typical Mexican vacation?). The following spring these same adults begin the dangerous return trip north. They themselves never make it to the prairies, but their progeny, deposited as eggs on milkweed plants, may. The small, ribbed eggs are about a millimeter (¹⁄₂₅ in.) in diameter. The chrysalis is a soft green color with gold spots, and a black and gold line about a third of the way down. This line is the suture along which the case will open when the butterfly emerges.

Monarch butterfly (*Danaus plexippus*)

Several generations may be born as the monarchs head north. The last generation born will be the one that journeys south again. Amazingly, although the same butterflies never make the round trip, somehow they know just where to go. The monarch is only one of four non-tropical species in the milkweed butterfly family, and the only one found on the prairies, although it is rarely seen in the Canadian prairies.

The caterpillars eat plants in the moderately toxic milkweed family, which renders both the caterpillars and the adults toxic to birds. As with so many brightly colored insects, their coloring means "don't eat me." Some butterflies, such as the viceroy, mimic the monarch coloring, but are not poisonous. The viceroy isn't even in the same family as the monarch.

Mourningcloak butterfly and spiny elm caterpillar (*Nymphalis antiopa*) (pp. 70, 112)

Green lattice or police car moth

Family Arctiidae
Gnophaela vermiculata

BUG AT A GLANCE
TYPE OF BUG: tiger moth
SIZE: wingspan 50 mm (2 in.)
WHAT IT LOOKS LIKE: triangular, black-and-white moth with two orange spots on the thorax near the head; caterpillar is yellow with black patches and has white hairs sprouting from blue dots, and a reddish brown head
WHERE YOU FIND IT: wherever host plants are found
WHEN YOU FIND IT: late July and August; daytime
WHAT IT EATS: adult may not feed at all; caterpillar specializes in eating the leaves of lungwort or any member of the borage family
FRIEND OR FOE: benign
WHAT TO DO: follow it until it lands on a flower and observe one of the prairies' prettiest moths

BUG BIO
This moth belongs to a group of tiger moths that fly by day. Members of this colorful family often sport orange, pink, black, or white markings. The daytime flight, plus its bright coloring, often makes people mistake it for a butterfly. It is not a strong flier, so you'd think it would be a sitting duck for sharp-eyed birds. Luckily, it is protected by its bright coloring, which usually means "Don't eat me, I taste bad" in the bird world. Birds learn this universal language very quickly and leave the moth to flap its erratic way through your garden.

Another insect in this family that you may recognize is the caterpillar of *Lophocampa maculata*, often called the woollybear (see p. 168).

Galium sphinx moth, bedstraw hawkmoth, or fireweed hawkmoth

Family Sphingidae
Hyles gallii

BUG AT A GLANCE (illustration p. 76)

TYPE OF BUG: sphinx or hawk moth

SIZE: wingspan up to 70 mm (2¾ in.); caterpillar is 60 mm (2½ in.) long

WHAT IT LOOKS LIKE: thick-bodied moth with narrow, tapered fore wings featuring a yellow stripe along the middle of the wing axis; large, hairless caterpillar has white spots along the sides, a red head, and a red horn on the hind end

WHERE YOU FIND IT: where host plants are found; attracted to light

WHEN YOU FIND IT: May to August; at night

WHAT IT EATS: caterpillar enjoys fireweed, woodruff, and bedstraw; adult eats nectar from flowers such as bouncing bet, lilac, and bee balm

FRIEND OR FOE: benign

WHAT TO DO: try to watch it sip nectar while it hovers

BUG BIO

The female lays her eggs on leaves of the host plants. Fully grown caterpillars pupate underground in a loose cocoon. There is one generation per year, which may be seen flying from May to August.

Members of this family are characterized by narrow, pointed wings that are held back at a sharp angle and small hind wings. The name "sphinx moth" comes from the sphinxlike pose that the caterpillar may assume. Some of these moths are active by day, and some are nocturnal.

Other sphinx moths that you may encounter in your garden include the one-eyed sphinx moth (*Smerinthus cerisyi*) and the great ash sphinx moth (*Sphinx chersis*). Another moth in this family is the snowberry clearwing moth (*Hamaris diffinis*). It has large, clear patches on the wings and looks something like a bee. Despite its common name, it is not a member of the clearwing moth family (Sessiidae).

Polyphemus moth

Family Saturniidae
Antheraea polyphemus, syn. *Telea polyphemus*

BUG AT A GLANCE (illustration p. 76)

TYPE OF BUG: giant silkworm moth

SIZE: wingspan up to 15 cm (6 in.)

WHAT IT LOOKS LIKE: huge moth with tan, beige, and rust-colored wings, with distinctive eyespots on hind wings and smaller eyespots on fore wings; it has a dark and light band along all wing margins; the enormous green caterpillars may have protuberances with spines and bristlelike hairs

WHERE YOU FIND IT: usually in wooded areas; attracted to light

WHEN YOU FIND IT: May to July; active at night; one generation

WHAT IT EATS: adult doesn't eat; caterpillar likes saskatoons or other members of the rose family, such as crabapples

FRIEND OR FOE: benign

WHAT TO DO: count yourself lucky to see such a beautiful moth

BUG BIO

The members of this family are large, striking moths with wings beautifully patterned like exotic tapestries. Silkworm moths live for a very short time, so when the adults emerge from their cocoons, mating must occur that evening or night. They lay their eggs right away, singly or in small groups, on host plants. There is only one generation on the prairies, flying from May to July.

Other species of saturniid moths that may be found in the prairie region include the Columbia silkmoth (*Hyalophora columbia*) and the cecropia silkmoth (*H. cecropia*).

Despite their silken cocoons, these moths are not used commercially for silk production. Silk moths are *Bombyx mori* (Family Bombicidae) and probably originated in Asia.

Galium sphinx moth, bedstraw hawkmoth (*Hyles gallii*) (p. 74)

Polyphemus moth (*Antheraea polyphemus*, syn. *Telea polyphemus*) (p. 75)

Underwing or owlet moths

Family Noctuidae
Subfamily Catocalinae

BUG AT A GLANCE (no illustration)

TYPE OF BUG: noctuid moth
SIZE: wingspan usually 20 to 45 mm (¾ to 1¾ in.)
WHAT THEY LOOK LIKE: well-camouflaged moth that holds its wings
rooflike over the body; hind wings are often brightly colored
WHERE YOU FIND THEM: everywhere; often attracted to light
WHEN YOU FIND THEM: most common in August and September; at night
WHAT THEY EAT: vegetation, depending on the species
FRIEND OR FOE: mainly benign
WHAT TO DO: if you want to see it, try the sugaring technique
described below to attract it to your garden

BUG BIO

Underwing moths are masters at camouflage. Most common in August
or September, they escape notice unless they reveal their brightly colored
hind wings. Revealing the hind wings is thought to startle a possible
predator sufficiently to allow the moth to escape. The caterpillars are also

Sugaring for Moths

You can attract night-flying moths using this time-tested, nineteenth-century technique.

First, mix up an aromatic paste of sugar (brown or white), some alcohol (beer, wine, etc.), a bit of malt vinegar, some old mashed fruit if you have it, and molasses. The paste should not be runny. Then, let it ferment for at least several days. There are many different recipes and some moth afficionados swear by their own, well-guarded secret formulae. You can experiment or look up recipes on the Internet.

At twilight, spread this paste on the bark of a tree at about chest height (a bit lower for your kids). Rough-barked trees are best.

Throughout the night, go out quietly with a flashlight and see what comes. You might not be successful every night, but don't be discouraged. Try sugaring on different evenings and at different times in August and September.

camouflage experts: they have uneven fringes on their sides that can hug tree bark, thus eliminating even a shadow that might expose them.

There may be more than four hundred species of underwing moths in North America. Gardeners are more likely to be familiar with the unruly offspring of a few related noctuid moths, such as the cutworm (see pp. 138–139).

Braconid wasps

Family Braconidae

BUG AT A GLANCE (illustration p. 80)

TYPE OF BUG: parasitoid wasps

SIZE: up to 7 mm (⅓ in.) long

WHAT THEY LOOK LIKE: brown, reddish brown, or black wasps that typically have rather short abdomens; small white cocoons may be visible on the husk of the host insect or "log-piled" with others on a leaf or twig

WHERE YOU FIND THEM: widely distributed, wherever host insects (often caterpillars) are found

WHEN YOU FIND THEM: spring to fall, depending on the species

WHAT THEY EAT: adults feed on nectar or the honeydew secretions of aphids; larvae feed parasitically within caterpillars or maggots

FRIEND OR FOE: friend

WHAT TO DO: have a nice cup of tea and let the wasp go about its work

BUG BIO

You may never notice these small, dark insects. Eggs are typically laid under the skin of a host insect. The host is rarely killed until the braconid larva is ready to pupate. Some species pupate outside the host, and others within it. When the adult wasp emerges, the host remains as a dry husk. Braconid wasps overwinter as larvae or pupae, depending on the species.

Fortunately, hosts targeted by braconid wasps are often insects that you do not want in your garden, such as aphids and caterpillars. A collection of empty aphid husks on a plant is a sign that braconids have paid a visit. These wasps tend to be very host-specific and scientists estimate that there may be forty thousand species worldwide, each with its own target host. Many species are deliberately employed as biological controls.

Ichneumon wasps

Family Ichneumonidae

BUG AT A GLANCE (illustration p. 80)
TYPE OF BUG: parasitoid wasps
SIZE: 5 to 30 mm (⅕ to 1¼ in.) long
WHAT THEY LOOK LIKE: brown to black, often brightly patterned
wasps, characterized by very long antennae which often have
white or yellow segments in the middle; many sport a very long
ovipositor at the back
WHERE YOU FIND THEM: widely distributed wherever host insects are
found; may be found at night around lights or screens
WHEN YOU FIND THEM: spring to fall, depending on the species
WHAT THEY EAT: adults feed on flower nectar; larvae feed on host
insects, commonly caterpillars, grubs, and maggots
FRIEND OR FOE: friend
WHAT TO DO: relax and remember that is not a stinger on its rear end

BUG BIO

The female lays her eggs on or inside a host insect. The larvae feed on the
insides of their host and then overwinter as pupae, still inside the host
insect. Adults eventually emerge from their pupal cases and their host.

Solitary ichneumon wasps are very like braconid wasps in that they
parasitize many insects. Several are not host-specific, indulging themselves with a smorgasbord of available hosts. Females possess a long
ovipositor, which looks alarmingly like a fierce stinger, but is in fact the
organ used to insert eggs into the host insect. There are about six thousand
species of ichneumon wasps in North America.

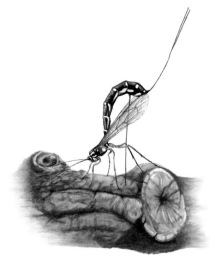

Ichneumon wasp (Family Ichneumonidae) (p. 79)

Braconid wasp (Family Braconidae) (p. 78)

Look at that Stinger!

Many female members of Order Hymenoptera have a long sharp-looking object protruding from the back end, which may be a stinger, or, alternatively, may be an ovipositor. An ovipositor is a tube that the female of many hymenopteran species, such as parasitic wasps, uses to lay her eggs within a host species or to bore through wood to get at fat, juicy grubs hiding beneath. A stinger is a modified ovipositor that is common among the sterile female workers of social hymenopterans like ants, vespid wasps, and honeybees. Since these workers are sterile, it is quite clear what this modified version is for.

Vespid Wasps (hornets, yellowjackets, paper wasps)

Family Vespidae

BUG AT A GLANCE

TYPE OF BUG: social wasps

SIZE: 8 to 25 mm (⅓ to 1 in.) long

WHAT THEY LOOK LIKE: typical, narrow-waisted wasps, with distinctive black-and-yellow or black-and-white stripes; wings are held straight by the sides, folded lengthwise, which is one way to tell them from bees

WHERE YOU FIND THEM: widely distributed; nests may be located in or near buildings, or underground

WHEN YOU FIND THEM: spring; numbers increase through to fall

WHAT THEY EAT: adults feed on a sweet liquid produced by the larva, plant nectar, and other sweets; adults feed chewed-up insect prey or scraps of meat to developing larvae

FRIEND OR FOE: friend of the garden, potential foe of gardeners

WHAT TO DO: if a nest is too close to human activity or if a family member is allergic to wasp venom, then eradicate the nest; otherwise, leave it alone

BUG BIO

The alarming black-and-yellow stripes and the narrow waist are all the clues you need to identify vespid wasps. The distinctive coloration is a well-known and respected signal meaning "stop or I'll sting." There are many different species of wasps in the vespid family, but gardeners are most concerned with the social ones.

In the spring a fertile queen, the only wasp to survive winter, emerges from her hibernation spot and begins to construct a nest. Some species, mainly those dubbed yellowjackets, construct an underground nest. Paper wasps and hornets build a strong and lightweight nest attached to tree branches or under eaves.

The nest, whether underground or attached to a tree, is constructed of paper, which the wasp creates by scraping bits of dead wood or paper and chewing it up with saliva. Inside the nest are paper "combs" with hexagonal cells in which the larvae live.

A nest begun by a single queen may eventually grow to have hundreds or thousands of inhabitants. After rearing an initial set of sterile female workers, the queen remains in the nest and spends the rest of her life laying eggs. The workers care for the eggs, larvae, and pupae within the nest and perform additional tasks, such as nest repair and expansion. When the nest reaches peak size in late summer, fertile males (drones) and fertile females (new queens) are produced.

The potentially aggressive nature of vespid wasps and their powerful sting are legitimate concerns for gardeners. Otherwise, these wasps are allies, controlling other insects and pollinating flowers. All wasps may become very aggressive near their nests.

In the fall, as prey becomes scarce, hornets and yellowjackets start to scavenge around open garbage cans, at picnics, and at other places where food and sweet drinks are found. They also become more aggressive. Their purpose in life is coming to an end, and all of the carefully orchestrated hive activities fall into disarray. By winter the nest is empty, and most of the wasps are dead. Only the newly mated queens survive. These queens find a place to hibernate, and the following spring, the whole cycle begins anew.

If you find it necessary to eradicate a nest, it is best to hire a reputable exterminator. Removing a nest can result in an attack from the occupants, and vespid wasps are very quick to respond to a threat.

To lessen the chances of an unpleasant encounter, you can:

- remove or block any new nests you discover before the queen gets too far along in her project
- employ a wasp trap in the fall if scavenging wasps become a problem
- keep exposed garbage and food to a minimum in the fall
- pick up and discard overripe fruit that has fallen from trees.
- avoid scented soaps, perfumes
- avoid wearing bright clothing

A Wasp Feeder

In late summer, when wasps become hungry and aggressive, consider putting out a wasp feeder. This is not for the wasps' benefit, since by winter they all die anyway. Place it far away from where you eat and sit outdoors, and the wasps will go there instead of crashing your Labor Day garden luncheon. Calgary gardener Anne Savannah puts out a shallow pan of sugary liquid (1 part sugar to 4 parts water) and even provides a sloping rock as a landing pad.

Bumblebees and honeybees

Family Apidae

BUG AT A GLANCE (illustration p. 84)

TYPE OF BUG: social bees

SIZE: up to 25 mm (1 in.) long

WHAT THEY LOOK LIKE: stout bees with yellow or orange and black markings; bumblebees (*Bombus* spp.) are stouter and hairier than honeybees (*Apis* spp.)

WHERE YOU FIND THEM: widely distributed; the more flowers in your garden, the more bees you'll get

WHEN YOU FIND THEM: spring; numbers increase through to fall

WHAT THEY EAT: bees feed on nectar and pollen; developing larvae are fed "bee bread" supplied by worker bees

FRIEND OR FOE: delightful friend

WHAT TO DO: encourage bees by having flowers in bloom from early spring till fall

BUG BIO

There are many species of bumblebees and one honeybee (*Apis mellifera*), all of them effective pollinators. Bumblebees (*Bombus* spp.) form annual colonies much like social wasps. Their colonies tend to be smaller than honeybee or wasp colonies, often numbering less than one hundred individuals. Some prairie bumblebees are 25 mm (1 in.) long. There are more species of bumblebees in northern climates than in southern ones.

A new queen emerges from hibernation in spring and proceeds to build a nest. After a sufficient number of worker bees are raised to adulthood, the

Bumblebee (Family Apidae)

queen stays in the nest and spends the rest of her life laying eggs. Unlike honeybees, worker bumblebees are sometimes able to lay infertile eggs that turn into males. Very persistent workers may try to usurp the queen, which can lead to head butting and leg-pulling contests, unexpectedly rowdy behavior from such seemingly placid creatures.

Male bees are born later in the season and do no work in the nest. They spend a few days eating nectar in the nest and then leave to live among the flowers until fertile new queens leave the nest to mate. After mating, all the bees, including the old, worn-out queen, die, except for the newly fertilized queens, who must gain enough weight to overwinter successfully. Having a good supply of late-blooming flowers in your garden is very helpful to these little friends.

Honeybees have a somewhat different social life. Their colonies can be long-lived. As old queens die, new ones take their place. After establishing her hive, a queen spends the rest of her life laying eggs, most of which will give rise to female workers, although in spring a small number of male drones are produced. The male's only purpose is to mate to ensure survival of the species. Until the day of the nuptial flight, the males just hang around and are fed and groomed by their sisters.

Female workers live about six weeks, and in the first part of their adult lives, go about doing chores in the hive, such as repairing tears in the hive and feeding the developing larvae. In the last part of their lives, they become foragers, going to and fro, bringing nectar and pollen back to the hive.

From time to time, some of the female honeybee larvae develop into queens. Females turn into queens when workers decide to feed them royal jelly their entire larval lives. Other larvae just get the royal jelly for three days and then are fed bee bread, a mixture of pollen and honey made by the worker bees. If more than one new queen is in the hive at any one time, the first emerging adult queen stings all other developing rivals. This sounds like poor play, but the shenanigans of some human royals in the past have also lacked decorum.

On a fine, clear day, when the new honeybee queens and the drones are ready, they emerge from the nest for their nuptial flight. Lucky males find a queen and mate successfully, but lose part of their abdomen in the process of pulling free after mating and soon die. Unsuccessful males return to their hive but become pariahs, shunned by their sisters who will no longer feed or groom them. When the weather turns cold, any surviving males are forcibly ejected from the nest to die. It's not much fun being a drone bee.

Successfully mated honeybee females return to their hive to begin their egg-laying lives. If the original queen is still there, she may leave with an entourage of workers and some drones in a swarm to establish a new hive. There is some debate about whether or not swarming bees are aggressive, but it is best to stay clear of them.

During the winter, bees huddle closely together and feed on stores of honey to survive. If they can keep themselves fed, warm, and clean, the hive will survive for another year. In the coldest climates, it may not be possible for bees to overwinter. The vast majority of prairie honeybees that we see are raised by beekeepers.

A Bee Dance

Living such social lives, you might think bees have a social life. Alas, this is not so. However, in 1923, Karl von Frisch made the discovery that, when honeybees find a good source of nectar, they do a dance in front of hive-mates, dubbed the "waggle dance." The waggle dance somehow explains to the watching bees where to find this new source of nectar.

8

THE CONIFER CROWD

The cast of characters you are likely to notice in your conifers are all very tiny and not the sort of visitors you want in your garden. You usually notice their effect on your conifers before you spot them. Fortunately, mature conifers are often tough enough to withstand their activities.

Pine needle scale

Chionaspis pinifoliae, syn. *Phenacaspis pinifoliae*

BUG AT A GLANCE (illustration p. 88)

  TYPE OF BUG: armored scale
  SIZE: about 3 mm (⅛ in.) long
  WHAT IT LOOKS LIKE: tiny, white, waxy disc on needles, oval and pointed at both ends; tiny, red crawler is rarely seen
  WHERE YOU FIND IT: pine or spruce needles
  WHEN YOU FIND IT: year-round; new scale develops in spring
  WHAT IT EATS: sucks sap from needles
  FRIEND OR FOE: a definite foe; causes needle loss and branch death
  WHAT TO DO: remove badly infected trees; predators such as lady beetles and parasitic wasps help with control

BUG BIO

Perversely, on the prairies pine needle scale appears mostly on spruce, not pine trees. Female scales are much larger than males and have no wings, eyes, or legs. The smaller males have wings but no mouths. In late summer they mate, after which the male dies. The female lays eggs under her own body and then dies. These eggs overwinter protected by her dead body.

The tiny, red crawlers that hatch from the eggs move a short distance along the needles for several days, looking for a place to feed. Wind can disperse them quite a distance to other trees. The crawlers then settle and secrete a protective white oval scale with pointed ends. These mature white scales are obvious on dark green needles.

Spruce and pine needles are stunted and trees may be disfigured by the sap-sucking activities of these little monsters. Severe infestations can cause a great deal of needle loss and may eventually kill the tree. Chemical controls are useful only on the crawler stage. Insecticides also kill enemies of scale, which can make the situation worse. Lady beetles and parasitic wasps eat scale insects.

Spruce gall adelgid

Adelges cooleyi

BUG AT A GLANCE (illustration of symptoms, p. 44)

    TYPE OF BUG: adelgid

    SIZE: 3 mm (⅛ in.) long

    WHAT IT LOOKS LIKE: small, wingless, flattened bug with a fluffy, white coat

    WHERE YOU FIND IT: spruce

    WHEN YOU FIND IT: woolly adelgids appear in early June; galls seen from July onward

    WHAT IT EATS: sucks sap from needles

    FRIEND OR FOE: minor foe; galls are unsightly, but cause little damage

    WHAT TO DO: remove the galls by hand if desired

BUG BIO

Spruce trees with hard, swollen brown tips on the branches have been attacked by woolly, aphidlike adelgids. In spring, overwintering nymphs develop into fluffy, wingless females called "stem mothers." After mating, each female lays one egg at a branch node. Young nymphs suck sap from the needles. These nymphs overwinter on the stems and begin feeding again in the spring at the branch tips, which causes galls to form around them. The galls begin as swollen branch tips that turn pink, then purple, and eventually brown over the summer. By midsummer, the mature nymphs emerge from the galls and become winged adults, which are reddish brown, wasplike insects.

These adelgids usually use Douglas fir as an alternate host. Winged adelgids emerging from the spruce galls in midsummer fly to Douglas fir trees, where they lay eggs on needles. Young nymphs emerge in late summer and overwinter at the base of needles. They are covered with white fluff and begin feeding again in the spring, but no galls are formed. In late summer, winged adults fly to spruce again. Where Douglas fir is not present, this adelgid can reproduce solely on spruce.

Galls persist for several years, but cause little damage. You can remove them in May or June if you consider them unattractive. It is possible to kill the woolly adelgids with a contact insecticide when they are visible on the tree, but they are there only for a short time and are often not noticed.

Pine needle scale (*Chionaspis pinifoliae*, syn. *Phenacaspis pinifoliae*) (p. 86)

White pine weevil

Pissodes strobi

BUG AT A GLANCE (illustration of symptoms, p. 41)

    TYPE OF BUG: weevil

    SIZE: larva is up to 10 mm (⅜ in.) long; adult is 7 mm (⅓ in.) long

    WHAT IT LOOKS LIKE: larva is a short, fat, white grub with a tan-colored head; adult is a dark brown or black beetle with patches of lighter brown and white, and a long, curved snout

    WHERE YOU FIND IT: spruce or pine

    WHEN YOU FIND IT: damage is evident in midsummer

    WHAT IT EATS: larva chews wood within the new leader of the tree; adult feeds on upper tree branches

    FRIEND OR FOE: foe; disfigures leaders (growing tips) of young trees

    WHAT TO DO: cut the leader down to the first set of branches below any sign of damage in the trunk

BUG BIO

White pine weevils occur more often on spruce trees than on pine trees on the prairies. Adults overwinter beneath the trees, emerge in spring, and lay eggs in wounds on last year's leader growth. Larvae feed in the tree's cambial layer. As the larvae mature, they form groups that can girdle a branch. After eating their fill, they pupate in cocoons beneath the bark. Adults bore holes through the bark and emerge in early fall. The telltale holes and dry, white drops of sap are indicators of weevil damage. The leaders of infested trees curl over like a shepherd's crook and gradually die.

Chemical controls for white pine weevil are not practical. Instead, remove the tops of infected trees well below the affected area. To improve the appearance of a tree, create a new "leader" by bending a branch upward, tying it to a support, and, in turn, tying the support to the trunk. Trees are not as likely to become infected as they mature.

Whitespotted sawyer

Monochamus scutellatus

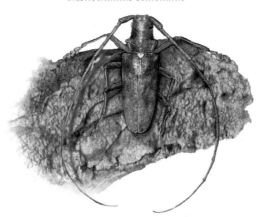

BUG AT A GLANCE

    TYPE OF BUG: long-horned beetle
    SIZE: larva is 40 mm (1½ in.) long; adult is 15 to 25 mm (⅝ to 1 in.) long
    WHAT IT LOOKS LIKE: narrow, black beetle with a white spot behind the head and very long antennae
    WHERE YOU FIND IT: dead or dying spruce or pine
    WHEN YOU FIND IT: adult seen in late June or July
    WHAT IT EATS: coniferous needles and bark

FRIEND OR FOE: benign in the garden; it eats only dead or dying material

WHAT TO DO: don't be afraid of such a little creature

BUG BIO

Male whitespotted sawyers have antennae twice as long as their body; females have antennae the same length as their body. Females lay eggs in slits made in the bark of dead trees or lumber in midsummer. Larvae emerge in about two weeks and begin feeding in the wood below the bark. Sawdust and wood chips are often visible below the tree. The larvae create oval holes to burrow deeper into the wood to spend the winter. In the spring, they emerge, feeding deep in the wood. The larvae grow to be 40 mm (1½ in.) long, with beige bodies and dark heads. They overwinter again and pupate the next spring. Adults emerge in late spring, feed on bark and needles for about ten days, then mate and lay eggs.

Whitespotted sawyers can do considerable damage to lumber and are a nuisance in stored firewood, but they do no harm to healthy trees.

Spruce budworm

Choristoneura fumiferana

BUG AT A GLANCE (illustration p. 92)

TYPE OF BUG: tortricid moth caterpillar

SIZE: larva is up to 25 mm (1 in.) long; adult wingspan is about 20 mm (¾ in.)

WHAT IT LOOKS LIKE: reddish brown caterpillar with dark head and white spots; adult is a small, grayish moth

WHERE YOU FIND IT: tips of spruce branches

WHEN YOU FIND IT: overwintered caterpillar appears in May; adult moth is seen in July

WHAT IT EATS: larva eats spruce needles

FRIEND OR FOE: foe; causes needle loss, starting at top of tree

WHAT TO DO: bacterial insecticides like BTk may be applied; encourage natural predation by other insects and spiders by avoiding the use of other pesticides

BUG BIO

Clusters of eggs are laid on spruce needles, and the emerging caterpillars move to cover amongst the needles. They overwinter as caterpillars in cracks in the bark and feed again in spring when the weather is warm. Spruce budworms start feeding on older needles of spruce trees, and then move to new needles, which are under the paper cap covering the tips of branches. The caterpillars molt five times before pupation, creating silky webs that incorporate debris from the tree. New webs are created in a different place with each molt. The caterpillars pupate in midsummer and, subsequently, small, gray adult moths emerge and mate.

Several predators eat the caterpillars, so consider carefully whether or not the use of insecticides is justified. Late spring and early fall frosts can kill large numbers of them. Spruce budworm is not common in the Calgary area but does occur in other parts of the prairies.

Yellow-headed spruce sawfly

Pikonema alaskensis

BUG AT A GLANCE (illustration p. 92)

TYPE OF BUG: sawfly

SIZE: larva is up to 20 mm (¾ in.) long; adult is 8 to10 mm (⅓ to ⅜ in.) long

WHAT IT LOOKS LIKE: small, green, caterpillarlike larva with yellow-orange head; adult is a tiny, reddish brown, flylike insect

WHERE YOU FIND IT: spruce

WHEN YOU FIND IT: larva appears mid to late June

WHAT IT EATS: larva eats spruce needles

FRIEND OR FOE: foe; can be a serious problem

WHAT TO DO: determine the severity of the infestation; hose down larvae with a hard spray of water; spray a contact insecticide if the infestation is severe

BUG BIO

The larvae of this sawfly overwinter in cocoons in the soil. In early June they form pupae and a few days later emerge as adults. Females deposit a single egg at the base of a needle. The eggs hatch in five to ten days, revealing small, yellowish green larvae with yellow-orange heads. The larvae feed on new needles and can also move to older foliage. If damage is confined to new needles, it does little harm to the tree. New buds are not affected and will grow normally into small branches the next year. If damage extends well into older needles, it becomes a more serious problem. Defoliation may be severe enough to affect the health of the tree.

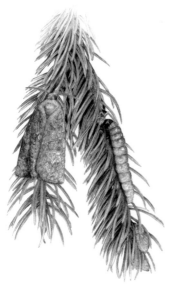

Trees are most commonly affected when they are several years old, until they reach a height of about 8 m (25 to 30 ft.). Birds help to control populations by eating the larvae. A hard spray of water with a garden hose may prove effective. If larvae numbers are very large and if they have moved beyond new needles to older growth, spraying with a contact insecticide may be worthwhile. A significant lack of green foliage means photosynthesis is drastically reduced, so severe infestations can cause serious harm to trees.

Spruce budworm
(*Choristoneura fumiferana*) (p. 90)

Yellowheaded spruce sawfly
(*Pikonema alaskensis*) (p. 91)

Webspinning sawfly

Cephalcia fascipennis

BUG AT A GLANCE (no illustration)
TYPE OF BUG: sawfly
SIZE: larva is up to 25 mm (1 in.) long; adult is about 15 mm (⅝ in.) long
WHAT IT LOOKS LIKE: small, caterpillarlike larva has black head and greenish brown body; brown or black adult is wasplike
WHERE YOU FIND IT: spruce and pine
WHEN YOU FIND IT: larva appears in June
WHAT IT EATS: larva eats pine and spruce needles; adult feeds on flowers
FRIEND OR FOE: minor foe
WHAT TO DO: hose down nests with a hard stream of water

BUG BIO

Overwintering adults emerge from the soil in the spring. Eggs are laid on the needles of trees. When the eggs hatch, groups of larvae feed together on needles. They spin protective, weblike nests that contain needles and sawdust known as frass in the crotches of trees. Damage is more cosmetic than harmful.

Spruce spider mite

Oligonychus ununguis

BUG AT A GLANCE

TYPE OF BUG: spider mite

SIZE: female is about 0.5 mm (⅟₅₀ in.) in diameter; male is smaller

WHAT IT LOOKS LIKE: very tiny, dark creature with eight legs; too small to see easily

WHERE YOU FIND IT: spruce and juniper

WHEN YOU FIND IT: larva first appears in mid-May; several generations

WHAT IT EATS: needle sap of spruce, occasionally of Douglas fir and juniper

FRIEND OR FOE: foe; causes needle loss, starting on lower branches

WHAT TO DO: hose webs frequently with hard spray of water; use miticide if infestation is severe

BUG BIO

Spruce spider mites are tiny, eight-legged creatures that are related to spiders. Their legs are so small, you need a magnifying glass to see them.

The mites spin a fine, dusty web around themselves for protection. They suck sap from needles of spruce and junipers, and occasionally other conifers, creating a speckled appearance on the needles, which eventually turn brown and fall off. Damage is most often found on the inside—on older needles—and it spreads upward to the outer parts of the tree.

Spider mites overwinter as eggs on branches, and juvenile mites emerge in early summer. They become adults very quickly and several generations can develop, each taking about two to three weeks to reach maturity. Mites are much more common in hot, dry weather, and can spread by wind.

If you suspect spider mites, hold a piece of white paper under a branch and tap the branch. If mites are present, some will fall to the paper and be seen scurrying away. Frequent hosing down of the tree will often keep mites under control. As a last resort, or if large amounts of water for hosing are not easily available, mite-killer sprays may be used. Insecticides don't work because these little guys are not insects.

9

THE DECIDUOUS TREE DENIZENS

Trees and shrubs are virtual condominiums and food fairs for a myriad of creatures. It is normal for them to house huge numbers of insects and their kin, and many insect-eating birds depend upon this feast. Insects, even pest species, seldom seriously bother healthy trees. On the other hand, trees are a long-term investment for gardeners. They clean our air and protect our gardens so it is prudent to deal with those instances in which a tree may need some help.

Black willow aphid

Pterocomma smithiae

BUG AT A GLANCE (no illustration)
  TYPE OF BUG: aphid
  SIZE: about 3.5 mm (⅛ in.) long
  WHAT IT LOOKS LIKE: large (as aphids go), black, flattened, oval insect, usually wingless, with distinctive orange projections extending from the rear end; found in clusters
  WHERE YOU FIND IT: young branches of willow and poplar trees
  WHEN YOU FIND IT: late summer
  WHAT IT EATS: sap of small branches
  FRIEND OR FOE: minor foe
  WHAT TO DO: hose down tree frequently with a hard spray of water

BUG BIO
Females lay yellow eggs in the fall on young willow and poplar branches. The eggs hatch in the spring and new aphids begin to suck sap through the soft bark, but do little damage on mature branches. Many generations are born live directly from the mature aphids and continue to live on the same branches. The aphids secrete sticky syrup called honeydew, which attracts wasps, ants, and sapsuckers. Sooty mold will also develop where they feed, giving the trees a dirty look.

Large, otherwise healthy trees will generally not be damaged by these aphids, as loss of small branches does little harm. A strong blast of water from the hose will help dislodge them. Large numbers of these aphids can cause premature leaf drop and reduce tree growth. Trees stressed by drought, such as windbreak trees, can lose vigor and suffer even more setbacks if the aphids are prolific. Unfortunately, if it is impractical to water acreage trees in very dry weather, it is also impractical to continually hose them down. You can try a contact insecticide, but remember, aphids are born pregnant. They will return.

Poplar petiole gall aphid

Pemphigus bursarius

BUG AT A GLANCE (illustration of symptoms, p. 44)
  TYPE OF BUG: aphid
  SIZE: 5 mm (⅕ in.) long
  WHAT IT LOOKS LIKE: flattened, oval, grayish white, wingless insect; some generations are dark colored; the root-living stage is a woolly, white aphid
  WHERE YOU FIND IT: hybrid poplars and lettuce
  WHEN YOU FIND IT: nymph is seen in late May
  WHAT IT EATS: poplar leaf petioles, lettuce
  FRIEND OR FOE: minor foe
  WHAT TO DO: don't grow lettuce near affected poplar trees; the galls don't damage the poplar

BUG BIO

These aphids need two hosts to complete their life cycle. Each aphid lays only one, very large egg on a poplar twig in the fall. The egg hatches when poplar leaves are opening in the spring. These newly hatched aphids are all wingless females. They move to the base of the leaves (the petioles), where they stimulate the growth of hollow galls by their feeding. A second winged generation is born to these females, and this new generation moves to lettuce plants, where they give birth directly to more aphids. As they feed on lettuce roots, they secrete a wax coating, which protects them from too much moisture. In the fall, a winged generation of males and females is born, which flies back to poplars to mate. The females produce one egg each, which overwinters, and next spring the whole weird life cycle begins again.

Another gall aphid, *Pemphigus populitransversus*, moves between cottonwood poplars and cruciferous plants such as cabbage, Brussels sprouts, cauliflower, and broccoli. *P. betae* alternates between balsam poplar and beets.

Petiole gall aphids aren't usually a serious problem unless you are growing vegetables commercially. Little damage is done to the poplar trees, but the generation that coats the roots of the secondary host anguishes the vegetable gardener. Because the vegetable has a hard time getting sufficient moisture, it may fail to develop properly and can wilt and die.

Honeysuckle aphid

Hyadaphis tataricae

BUG AT A GLANCE (illustration of symptoms, p. 41)

TYPE OF BUG: aphid
SIZE: 5 mm (⅕ in.) long
WHAT IT LOOKS LIKE: pinhead-sized, soft-bodied, wingless green insect with a whitish, powdery covering
WHERE YOU FIND IT: some varieties of honeysuckle shrubs
WHEN YOU FIND IT: first seen in late May; occurs all summer
WHAT IT EATS: sucks sap from honeysuckle leaves
FRIEND OR FOE: obnoxious foe; causes leaf and branch disfigurement
WHAT TO DO: trim new growth continuously; choose resistant varieties of honeysuckle

BUG BIO

Honeysuckle aphids were introduced into the prairies from Asia, via eastern North America. Saliva released during feeding causes very dense deformities called witches' brooms on some varieties of honeysuckle. The leaves curl up and the branch tip curls over. These very unsightly witches' brooms remain on the branches over the winter. The aphids overwinter in them as eggs or adults. Eggs hatch in mid-spring; all hatchlings are female, capable of giving birth to more live, pregnant, female aphids. No wonder they are difficult to eliminate. In the summer they are covered with a white, woolly material. In the fall males and females are produced to mate.

No contact insecticide can penetrate the dense growth of witches' brooms. The only control is to prune them off as they appear. Some honeysuckle varieties, such as climbing honeysuckle, 'Clavey's Dwarf', and 'Arnold's Red', are immune to this aphid, whereas many cultivars of Tatarian honeysuckle are very susceptible.

Woolly elm aphid

Eriosoma americanum

BUG AT A GLANCE (illustration p. 100)
TYPE OF BUG: woolly aphid
SIZE: 5 mm (⅕ in.) long
WHAT IT LOOKS LIKE: bluish black, flattened, oval insect with a white, woolly coat
WHERE YOU FIND IT: in curled leaves on American elm trees; in soil at base of saskatoon shrubs
WHEN YOU FIND IT: damage is first seen in early June; two generations
WHAT IT EATS: sap of American elm trees and roots of saskatoons (*Amelanchier* spp.)
FRIEND OR FOE: foe; causes leaf disfigurement
WHAT TO DO: hose down with a hard spray of water frequently; encourage the presence of aphid-eating lady beetles by not spraying insecticides

BUG BIO
The woolly elm aphid overwinters as an egg. Nymphs, all female, emerge in spring. These aphids suck sap from elm leaves, causing the leaves to curl, thereby protecting the aphids. Insecticides at this point will not be effective, as they can't reach the insects inside the rolled-up leaves. This generation matures as wingless adults, which then produce more female aphids. This second generation lives in dense colonies, secreting white, powdery wax and sticky honeydew. In midsummer, darker, winged female aphids are produced, which fly to seedling saskatoon shrubs. They move down the shrub stems and develop colonies that attack the shrub's fine roots. Secretions of the aphids turn the soil blue. In the fall, more winged aphids migrate back to elms where they produce a male and female generation. They mate, deposit eggs in the cracks of the tree bark, and die.

Lecanium scale

Lecanium corni, syn. *Eulecanium corni*

BUG AT A GLANCE (illustration p. 100)

TYPE OF BUG: soft scale

SIZE: 3 mm (⅛ in.) long

WHAT IT LOOKS LIKE: a hard, brown, half-sphere that can easily be scraped off bark; crawler is too small to be noticed

WHERE YOU FIND IT: branches of fruit trees, dogwood, birch, ash, and rose bushes

WHEN YOU FIND IT: year-round; new scale develops in July

WHAT IT EATS: sap from leaves and small branches

FRIEND OR FOE: foe; distorts leaves, may cause small branch and twig death

WHAT TO DO: remove affected branches

BUG BIO

It is difficult to recognize these hard, brown lumps as insects as they have no visible body parts and don't appear to move. For this reason, they can become very abundant before they are acknowledged as a pest. In early summer, males and females emerge, mate, and lay eggs, which remain under the female's body. In late July, flat-bodied crawlers emerge and move to leaves, where they feed until fall. Before winter, they move to twigs and small branches, where they secrete a scale over themselves. Large numbers of these scales can weaken affected trees and kill small branches, but a healthy tree is rarely in danger.

Scurfy scale

Chionaspis furfura

BUG AT A GLANCE (illustration p. 100)

TYPE OF BUG: armored scale

SIZE: 2 to 3 mm (¹⁄₁₀ to ⅛ in.) long

WHAT IT LOOKS LIKE: white, pear-shaped female is much larger than the slender male

WHERE YOU FIND IT: small branches of aspen, elm, ash, and other deciduous trees and shrubs

WHEN YOU FIND IT: year-round; new scale develops in spring
WHAT IT EATS: sap of twigs and branches
FRIEND OR FOE: foe; causes twig or branch death
WHAT TO DO: remove affected branches; dormant oil or other insecticides can only be used on crawlers

BUG BIO

Eggs overwinter on bark under the shell of the dead female. As with other scales, there is a crawler stage for a short time after the eggs hatch in the spring.

Although the white scales are relatively easy to see, the short-lived crawler stage is not usually observed. Pesticides are only useful on crawlers, but it is wiser to leave crawler control to their natural predators.

Scurfy scale (*Chionaspis furfura*)
(p. 99)

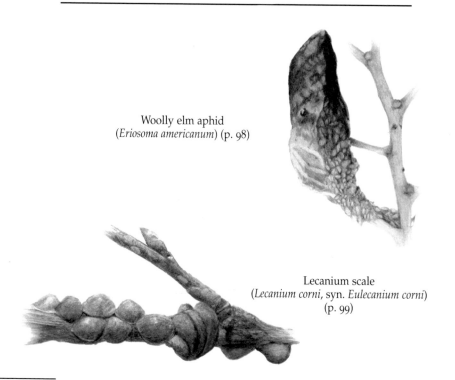

Woolly elm aphid
(*Eriosoma americanum*) (p. 98)

Lecanium scale
(*Lecanium corni*, syn. *Eulecanium corni*)
(p. 99)

Oystershell scale

Lepidosaphes ulmi

BUG AT A GLANCE

TYPE OF BUG: armored scale

SIZE: 3 mm (⅛ in.) long

WHAT IT LOOKS LIKE: an elongated, hard, brown shell, like a tiny oyster

WHERE YOU FIND IT: branches of cotoneaster, lilac, fruit trees, ash, and elm

WHEN YOU FIND IT: year-round; new scale develops in spring

WHAT IT EATS: sucks sap under bark

FRIEND OR FOE: foe

WHAT TO DO: remove affected branches; pesticides, such as oils, soap, or contact insecticides are useful only on crawlers

BUG BIO

Female oystershell scales are larger than males, have no wings, legs, or eyes, and are covered with a waxlike material. Males develop thin shells and emerge as two-winged insects with no mouthparts. They disappear after mating in the spring. The females lay eggs and die when it gets cold. Their dead bodies protect the eggs until the crawlers hatch in the spring and move to a suitable place on the host plant to feed. Talk about motherly devotion. They are often blown by wind or carried on animal fur or human clothing to new trees. When they find a good feeding site, they insert their mouthparts into bark to begin feeding.

Pesticides are useful only on crawlers, which are visible for a very short time. Pesticides also kill enemies of scale—lady beetles and parasitic wasps eat crawlers—which can make the situation worse.

Ash plant bug

Tropidosteptes amoenus

BUG AT A GLANCE (illustration p. 104)

TYPE OF BUG: plant bug
SIZE: 5 mm (⅕ in.) long
WHAT IT LOOKS LIKE: sturdy, flattened, rectangular bug, tan colored, with a triangular white patch on the back
WHERE YOU FIND IT: green ash and related species
WHEN YOU FIND IT: nymph first seen in early June
WHAT IT EATS: pierces leaf tissue and sucks sap from leaves
FRIEND OR FOE: minor foe
WHAT TO DO: hose tree down frequently; use contact insecticide only if infestation is severe and you can see the bugs

BUG BIO

The young nymphs of the ash plant bug emerge in the spring. They feed on the underside of leaves, molt several times, and become adults in mid-summer. The females lay eggs in slits in the bark. There are two generations; individuals of the second generation remain active until frost occurs and then overwinter inside the bark.

Ash plant bugs suck sap from the undersides of leaves, making the leaves mottled and spotty. Their black excrement is often visible on the leaves. If numbers of bugs are very high, they can cause foliage to appear scorched and sometimes drop, but most often, trees are merely unsightly. As long as there is sufficient green leaf surface for photosynthesis to take place, the trees will survive.

Bronze birch borer

Agrilus anxius

BUG AT A GLANCE (illustration p. 104)

TYPE OF BUG: wood-boring or jewel beetle

SIZE: 7 to 11 mm (⅓ to ½ in.) long

WHAT IT LOOKS LIKE: larva has a dark head and white body, and is rarely seen; adult beetle is long, narrow, and greenish black with a metallic sheen

WHERE YOU FIND IT: birch

WHEN YOU FIND IT: damage is seen from July onward

WHAT IT EATS: larva eats wood layer beneath birchbark; adult eats leaves

FRIEND OR FOE: foe; may kill upper branches

WHAT TO DO: remove dead wood; keep trees well watered; natural predators will help

BUG BIO

Adult beetles emerge in June. Females are strong fliers and search for places to lay eggs, usually in cracks in the bark on the sunny side of weak or dying trees. Larvae burrow into the cambial layer beneath the bark, excavating tunnels. The tree grows new wood over the tunnels, creating obvious lumpy areas on the branches. The larvae pupate in the sapwood. Adults chew D-shaped exit holes and overwinter in wood beneath the birchbark.

Bronze birch borer is not common on the prairies. When tops of birch trees die, it is much more likely from lack of water the previous fall. However, it is good to know how to recognize these beetles, and the effect they can have on your trees. The upper branches of birch are tunneled first and, when the branches are girdled with tunnels, they quickly die. Severe infestations can kill the whole tree. There is no practical control. Keeping trees healthy is the best thing you can do. Birch trees need ample water throughout the summer and fall. Birds, insects, and spiders eat the eggs, larvae, and beetles of bronze birch borers.

Ash plant bug (*Tropidosteptes amoenus*) (p. 102)

Bronze birch borer (*Agrilus anxius*) (p. 103)

Poplar borer

Saperda calcarata

BUG AT A GLANCE (no illustration)

TYPE OF BUG: long-horned beetle

SIZE: larva is up to 50 mm (2 in.) long; adult is 20 to 30 mm (¾ to 1¼ in.) long

WHAT IT LOOKS LIKE: larva is white with a brown head, grublike and legless; adult is a slender, gray beetle with yellowish orange markings and long antennae

WHERE YOU FIND IT: trembling aspen, cottonwood, and balsam poplar

WHEN YOU FIND IT: adult first seen on leaves in July; larval damage seen from early spring onward

WHAT IT EATS: larva feeds on wood beneath the bark of poplar; adult feeds on the leaves

FRIEND OR FOE: foe; weakens trees by boring, allowing decay to set in

WHAT TO DO: insert wire into hole to kill larvae; remove badly infected trees

BUG BIO

Adults lay eggs in C-shaped cuts in the tree bark and seal them in. The larvae feed on the inner layer of bark and sapwood and overwinter there, emerging in spring. They extend their feeding area into tree centers in the second year. The fine wood fiber that falls from exit holes is known as frass. Larval feeding can last for one or two years. Pupation occurs in the larval tunnels and adults emerge from the tree in early summer.

Adults feed on the young leaves of aspen and balsam poplar. Both trunks and root crowns can suffer damage, as well. Affected trees often exude large amounts of dark brown, sticky sap, which stains the tree trunk. Individual trees are often attacked continuously, yet their invaders do not usually kill them. Woodpeckers riddle trees with holes while looking for insects, which creates openings for fungus to establish under the bark and rot the trunk. Trees weakened by burrowing and woodpecker activity may fall over in windstorms.

Cottonwood leaf beetle

Chrysomela scripta

BUG AT A GLANCE (illustration p. 108)

TYPE OF BUG: leaf beetle

SIZE: larva is about 12 mm (½ in.) long; adult beetle is 8 mm (⅓ in.) long

WHAT IT LOOKS LIKE: larva is cream colored with black spots and resembles a lady beetle larva; adult has black head and yellow wing covers with seven elongated, black spots

WHERE YOU FIND IT: willow and poplar trees

WHEN YOU FIND IT: adult begins feeding in early June, larva in late June

WHAT IT EATS: larva eats leaves of most poplars, except aspen; adult eats leaves, leaving small, circular holes

FRIEND OR FOE: minor foe

WHAT TO DO: hose tree down with a hard spray of water; lady beetles eat eggs and larvae

BUG BIO

Cottonwood leaf beetles are seen in the spring when new leaves are emerging. They lay their eggs under leaves. The larvae feed on leaves for several weeks and then pupate. The pupae hang from leaves and adults emerge in a week. Adults overwinter in debris under trees.

Larvae can strip trees of leaves but new ones usually replace them, as it is early in the season. A good hosing may be in order if you observe a large number of larvae.

Aspen leaf beetles (*Chrysomela crotchi*) are similar to cottonwood leaf beetles but feed on aspens. The beetles are light brown or copper colored.

Willow leaf beetles (*Calligrapha multipunctata multipunctata*) eat willow foliage; they are spotted in an irregular pattern.

Western ash bark beetle

Hylesinus californicus

BUG AT A GLANCE (illustration of symptoms, p. 36)
    TYPE OF BUG: bark beetle
    SIZE: larva is 2 to 4 mm (⅒ to ⅛ in.) long; adult is about 3 mm (⅛ in.) long
    WHAT IT LOOKS LIKE: adult is brown and white variegated beetle; larva is a C-shaped, legless white grub with a brown head
    WHERE YOU FIND IT: ash trees in southern half of the prairie provinces and in the northern plains of the United States
    WHEN YOU FIND IT: damage to bark is seen in spring and throughout the summer
    WHAT IT EATS: larva and adult eat inner wood of ash trees
    FRIEND OR FOE: minor foe
    WHAT TO DO: remove dead or dying branches; a sticky, adhesive band on tree trunk to trap bugs may be partially effective

BUG BIO

Adult beetles overwinter in holes in ash bark near the ground. They emerge in spring and crawl or fly up the tree. After mating, the females lay their eggs in horizontal rows just below the bark of dying or weakened tree branches. The larvae feed below the bark until mid-July. Rings of small ventilation holes that look like a bracelet are seen around an affected branch. Sap oozes out of these holes, and the bark becomes cracked, discolored, and rough. The first sign of damage is often yellow, wilting leaves as the tree cannot move fluids along the branch past the barrier created by feeding bugs. The larvae pupate in mid-July. Adults emerge in early fall and move to new branches until late fall, feeding beneath the bark. Their last task for the year is to bore galleries for eggs and larvae. They then crawl or fly down the tree to overwinter in debris beneath the tree.

    Western ash bark beetle is native to the prairies and is a concern on ash trees, most often on green ash. Mountain ash is in a completely different family of trees and is not susceptible.

Cottonwood leaf beetle
(*Chrysomela scripta*) (p. 106)

Native elm bark beetle

Hylurgopinus rufipes

BUG AT A GLANCE   (no illustration)

TYPE OF BUG: bark beetle

SIZE: adult and larva are each about 3 mm (⅛ in.) long

WHAT IT LOOKS LIKE: small, dark brown to black, shiny beetle with a spine on the underside of the abdomen; larva is a white, legless grub with a tan-colored head

WHERE YOU FIND IT: elm trees

WHEN YOU FIND IT: overwintering adult seen in mid-May; overwintering larva emerges in July

WHAT IT EATS: larva and adult eat wood of elm trees

FRIEND OR FOE: serious foe; it is the vector for the deadly Dutch elm disease (DED) fungus, *Ophiostoma ulmi*

WHAT TO DO: remove dead and dying trees; prune dead and dying limbs; do not store elm firewood; monitor elm trees diligently; report occurrences to authorities

BUG BIO

This beetle overwinters as a larva under the bark of elm trees and emerges in the spring when the trees have leafed out. The larva feeds at twig crotches, creating tunnels along the wood grain. At this point an otherwise healthy elm tree may be infected with the Dutch elm disease (DED) fungus. As mature beetles fly between infected and non-infected elm trees at breeding time, more trees become infected.

First symptoms of DED are wilting foliage and yellow, flagging leaves. The disease kills trees very quickly, so report any suspicious symptoms to appropriate authorities in your area. Alberta hosts some of the last healthy stands of elm trees in North America.

The smaller European elm bark beetle (*Scolytus multistriatus*) is an introduced relative that is also a serious vector of DED, although it is not common on the prairies.

Rose curculio

Merhynchites bicolor

BUG AT A GLANCE
TYPE OF BUG: weevil
SIZE: larva is 1 mm (½₅ in.) long; adult is 8 mm (⅓ in.) long
WHAT IT LOOKS LIKE: adult is a bright red beetle with a long snout; larva is a legless, whitish maggot
WHERE YOU FIND IT: mostly on shrub roses
WHEN YOU FIND IT: adult is first seen in June; larva may be seen in late June
WHAT IT EATS: larva eats seeds inside rose hips; adult eats pollen within developing flower buds
FRIEND OR FOE: foe to rose growers
WHAT TO DO: remove affected buds and hips

BUG BIO
The rose curculio overwinters as a larva in the soil. It pupates in spring and emerges as an adult in early summer when roses are budding. The adult feeds on flower buds, chewing holes in petals and buds to reach

pollen. The female punctures a rose hip and lays an egg in it. A larva then hatches and feeds on seeds inside the hip. Upon maturity, larvae fall to the ground and hibernate during winter.

Evidence that rose curculios are making a living on your roses is the failure of flower buds to open. Buds that do survive have many small holes in them. The shrub is not harmed but flowers are fewer and not as attractive. Remove affected buds to cut down on curculio numbers, and remove all hips to eliminate next year's generation.

Carpenterworm

Prionoxystus robiniae

BUG AT A GLANCE (no illustration)

TYPE OF BUG: carpenter moth caterpillar

SIZE: caterpillar is 50 to 70 mm (2 to 2¾ in.) long; female adult wingspan is 75 mm (3 in.)

WHAT IT LOOKS LIKE: caterpillar is usually greenish white with a brown head, some are pinkish with brown spots and a brown head; adult is a mottled gray moth; male adult is much smaller than the female

WHERE YOU FIND IT: 'Northwest' and other hybrid poplars

WHEN YOU FIND IT: caterpillar is seen in mid-June, poplar damage is seen in August

WHAT IT EATS: caterpillar eats wood inside trees; adult rarely feeds

FRIEND OR FOE: foe; weakens tree by tunneling

WHAT TO DO: kill larvae by inserting a wire into bored holes; if timed correctly, insecticides can be applied; remove loose, damaged bark, a preferred place for laying eggs

BUG BIO

Carpenterworms take three or four years to mature. The caterpillars move around on the tree for a short time and then tunnel into the cambial layer. They enlarge the tunnels as they grow. Frass that is ejected from the holes to keep the tunnels clean becomes noticeable by the end of the first summer. During the next two years, a maze of tunnels is formed and more frass collects at the base of the tree. Caterpillars may move to the outer trunk surface for a short time and then re-enter the tunnels. The small holes in trunks and branches are obvious. Caterpillars pupate in special chambers in spring of the fourth or fifth year, and adults appear in early summer.

Carpenterworms usually attack unhealthy trees. The caterpillars ingest a lot of wood, so trees are disfigured and dead branches or tops are common. Tunneling weakens trunks, and trees are easily blown over in windstorms. Since eggs are often laid in wounded bark, remove loose bark on trees so there is no place for eggs to be laid. Trees with serious infestations should be removed.

Uglynest caterpillar

Archips cerasivorana

BUG AT A GLANCE (illustration p. 112)

    TYPE OF BUG: tortricid moth caterpillar

    SIZE: caterpillar is 19 mm (¾ in.) long; adult wingspan is 20 to 24 mm (¾ to 1 in.)

    WHAT IT LOOKS LIKE: caterpillar is yellow-green with a shiny, dark head; adult is a small, pale brown moth

    WHERE YOU FIND IT: mostly on chokecherry, but also on other fruit trees

    WHEN YOU FIND IT: caterpillar is seen in early June

    WHAT IT EATS: leaves and fruit

    FRIEND OR FOE: minor foe; makes trees unsightly

    WHAT TO DO: destroy nests with a strong blast of water or disturb them with a stick

BUG BIO

Because uglynest caterpillars are ordinary looking, they are much easier to identify by their nests. They build their nests by tying leaves together with silk to form a safe, enclosed place, then feed on leaves and fruit inside this little fortress. In early fall, they pupate within the nests and a little later the pale brown moths emerge. They overwinter as eggs on trunks and branches of trees. Eggs hatch in the spring as the leaves emerge and the larvae immediately begin feeding on them.

Uglynest caterpillars can defoliate shrubs and trees, but the trees usually grow more leaves. Although they are weakened, trees and shrubs rarely die from infestations.

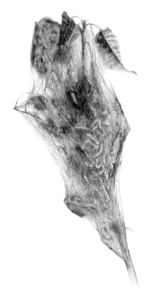

Uglynest caterpillar (*Archips cerasivorana*) (p. 111)

Spiny elm caterpillar

Nymphalis antiopa

BUG AT A GLANCE (illustration p. 72)

TYPE OF BUG: nymphalid butterfly caterpillar

SIZE: up to 50 mm (2 in.) long

WHAT IT LOOKS LIKE: caterpillar is black and bristly, with white speckles and a row of red spots on the back; tends to feed in groups, which makes it conspicuous

WHERE YOU FIND IT: elm, willow, aspen, and birch

WHEN YOU FIND IT: caterpillar is first seen in mid-June

WHAT IT EATS: elm, willow, aspen, and birch leaves

FRIEND OR FOE: friend and foe, depending on your philosophy

WHAT TO DO: surely it is worth sacrificing a few leaves, knowing that this caterpillar turns into a beautiful mourningcloak butterfly; remove egg clusters if numerous; parasitic wasps and birds eat larvae; spray bacterial insecticides like BTk

BUG BIO

These caterpillars are the larvae of the mourningcloak butterfly (see p. 70). They overwinter as butterflies in sheltered areas, and in early summer, lay clusters of cylindrical, ribbed, orange eggs on small tree branches. The caterpillars that hatch feed together in large groups and can defoliate a whole branch at once. They cause little permanent damage, but it may be wise to remove some egg clusters if they are numerous. If the infestation is severe, you can spray with an insecticide such as BTk.

Cartesian Caterpillars

Caterpillars of the geometrid moths are often called spanworms, loopers, measuring worms, or inchworms because of their characteristic movement—they bring their rear end up to the front, making a vertical loop of the body before moving the front end forward. Some imaginative person must have thought that these caterpillars looked as if they were making measurements of the earth, hence, the family name Geometridae.

Bruce spanworm

Operophtera bruceata

BUG AT A GLANCE (no illustration)

TYPE OF BUG: geometrid moth caterpillar

SIZE: caterpillar is 18 mm (¾ in.) long; adult male wingspan is 25 to 30 mm (1 to 1¼ in.)

WHAT IT LOOKS LIKE: fat, green, "looper" caterpillar with three light-colored, lengthwise stripes and a dark head; small male moth is gray with brown markings; the female moth is wingless

WHERE YOU FIND IT: native aspen

WHEN YOU FIND IT: caterpillar is seen in early June

WHAT IT EATS: aspen leaves

FRIEND OR FOE: minor foe

WHAT TO DO: no control usually necessary; use BTk if infestation is severe

BUG BIO

The caterpillars tie leaves together with silk, which is easily visible in early summer. They feed on leaves until close to the end of June, when they drop on threads and pupate in leaf litter on the ground under the tree. Adults emerge in fall and lay their eggs in bark cracks or beneath the tree. Eggs hatch in spring. The damage Bruce spanworms do is not enough to harm the tree and outbreaks usually last only a few years.

Fall cankerworm

Alsophila pometaria

BUG AT A GLANCE (illustration p. 116)

TYPE OF BUG: geometrid moth caterpillar

SIZE: 25 mm (1 in.) long

WHAT IT LOOKS LIKE: caterpillar is pale green with faint white, longitudinal lines; adult is a small, gray moth; female moths are wingless

WHERE YOU FIND IT: apple, poplar, elm, ash, and boxelder (Manitoba maple)

WHEN YOU FIND IT: caterpillar appears from early June to mid-July; adult appears in fall

WHAT IT EATS: leaves of host trees

FRIEND OR FOE: foe

WHAT TO DO: hose tree down with a hard spray of water; use a sticky band around the trunk to trap females; spray with BTk; birds, spiders, and some insects eat larvae

BUG BIO

Fall cankerworm is the caterpillar of a small moth that flies in the fall. These caterpillars belong to a group often called loopers or inchworms. Moths lay eggs in the fall on small branches. Caterpillars emerge in May and feed on the underside of new leaves. Holes in leaves are small at first, but older larvae eat the whole leaf except the midrib. By early summer the satiated caterpillars fall to the ground on silky threads, burrow into the soil under the tree, and pupate. They emerge in October, and the male moths fly, searching for females. Females climb tree trunks, mate, and lay eggs on branches, where they overwinter.

Spring cankerworm (*Paleacrita vernata*) is not as common on the prairies, but it does attack boxelders (Manitoba maples) and elms in the eastern prairies. These caterpillars are darker in color and overwinter as mature larvae. They pupate in early spring; females emerge in a few days and lay eggs in clusters on lower branches. Their feeding pattern is similar to that of the fall cankerworm.

Cankerworms can be killed with contact insecticides, but these poisons might kill their predators, too. A hard spray of water from the hose might be enough to dislodge them. A sticky band placed around the trunk of the tree will trap the females as they crawl up the tree.

Forest tent caterpillar

Malacosoma disstria

BUG AT A GLANCE (illustration p. 116)
TYPE OF BUG: lappet moth caterpillar
SIZE: 45 to 50 mm (1¾ to 2 in.) long
WHAT IT LOOKS LIKE: mature caterpillar is brown with blue stripes and a lengthwise row of white, keyhole-shaped dots; adult is a tan-colored moth
WHERE YOU FIND IT: tree branches, walls, roads, and sidewalks
WHEN YOU FIND IT: caterpillar is seen from early June to early July
WHAT IT EATS: leaves of aspen, birch, green ash, mayday, boxelder (Manitoba maple), elm, poplar, and fruit trees
FRIEND OR FOE: foe
WHAT TO DO: remove egg bands and silk pads; break webs up with a stick and leave for wasps and other predators; spray with BTk

BUG BIO
Tent caterpillars overwinter as eggs, and the small, black, hairy larvae hatch in early spring. They create silky mats to rest on when not feeding on leaves. In five or six weeks, the caterpillars form a cocoon on tree branches. The moths emerge in about ten days. They live only long enough to lay shiny, dark bands of eggs around small branches. The eggs are covered with foam that changes from silver to brown. The larvae emerge the following spring.

Forest tent caterpillars cluster together and can defoliate trees in a very short time. Because infestations occur early in the season, trees will generally produce new leaves, but several years of leaf loss can cause

Fall cankerworm (*Alsophila pometaria*) (p. 114)

Forest tent caterpillar (*Malacosoma disstria*) (p. 115)

twig death. In years of severe outbreaks, the larvae can cover trees, sides of houses, and sidewalks, making outdoor strolls unpleasant. A contact insecticide will kill the caterpillars it contacts, but often there are far too many to make spraying successful. Outbreaks are cyclical and usually last for about four or five years. Although outbreaks aren't pleasant, they are not particularly harmful.

Western tent caterpillar (*Malacosoma californicum pluviale*) also produces large tents. These caterpillars have orange hairs and black bodies with deep yellow, irregular spots. They feed mostly on fruit trees, particularly Schubert chokecherry.

Great ash sphinx moth caterpillar

Sphinx chersis

BUG AT A GLANCE

TYPE OF BUG: sphinx moth caterpillar

SIZE: up to 75 mm (3 in.) long; adult wingspan is 90 to 130 mm (3½ to 5 in.)

WHAT IT LOOKS LIKE: huge, pale green, smooth-skinned caterpillar with white, diagonal lines on its sides, and a "horn" on the rear end; adult is a large-bodied, grayish brown moth

WHERE YOU FIND IT: caterpillar is usually seen on lawns, sidewalks, etc.; nocturnal moths may be attracted to light at night

WHEN YOU FIND IT: caterpillar appears in July

WHAT IT EATS: caterpillar eats leaves of various trees, especially ash, lilac, and aspen; adult drinks nectar from tubular flowers such as nicotiana, petunia, and honeysuckle

FRIEND OR FOE: benign; a curiosity

WHAT TO DO: appreciate its unique appearance

BUG BIO

These caterpillars live in trees when young, eating leaves, although not to a noticeable extent. Manchurian ash is a favorite, but they also feed on lilac and aspen. Caterpillars fall or crawl to the ground when mature in August to find a suitable place to pupate. At this time they do not eat, but this is when most people notice them. They pupate and overwinter underground, about 120 mm (4¾ in.) beneath the soil surface. The moths appear in spring. Sphinx moths have long, sucking tubes that enable them to suck nectar from tubular flowers.

Sphinx moth larvae are often mistakenly called tomato hornworms, to which they are related. The tomato hornworm (*Manduca quinquemaculata*) is much less common on the prairies. Tobacco hornworm (*M. sexta*), which is common in the east, is also a member of the same family.

Aspen leaf roller

Pseudexentera oregonana

BUG AT A GLANCE (illustration of symptoms, p. 37)
   TYPE OF BUG: tortricid moth caterpillar
   SIZE: larva is 15 mm (⅝ in.) long; adult wingspan is 15 to 24 mm
   (⅝ to ¾ in.)
   WHAT IT LOOKS LIKE: caterpillar is cream colored, with a brown
   head; adult is a small, light yellow moth
   WHERE YOU FIND IT: caterpillar rolls up in leaves of aspen trees;
   nocturnal adult may be seen around lights at night
   WHEN YOU FIND IT: caterpillar is active in spring
   WHAT IT EATS: caterpillar eats aspen leaves
   FRIEND OR FOE: minor foe
   WHAT TO DO: ignore it as it does little harm and insecticides cannot
   reach it when it is rolled in a leaf; rolled leaves are best left on the
   tree since they are still useful for photosynthesis

BUG BIO
Aspen leaf rollers overwinter in the pupal stage and emerge in spring.
The moths mate and the females lay eggs on leaves and bark. When the
caterpillars hatch, they roll up the edges of the leaves and sometimes
even tie them, like a sleeping bag. The caterpillars are protected inside,
safe from insecticides or predators. Affected trees appear to have fewer
leaves because rolled-up leaves take up less room. They are, however,
perfectly useful leaves. Damage to trees is usually minimal and can
safely be ignored.

   Many other leaf rollers are found on the prairies. They affect different
trees, mostly willow, balsam poplar, boxelder (Manitoba maple), and
birch. These trees are all affected in much the same way. Except for the
displeasing look of affected trees, no harm is done.

Birch leafminer

Fenusa pusilla

BUG AT A GLANCE (illustration of symptoms, p. 37)

TYPE OF BUG: sawfly

SIZE: larva is up to 7 mm (⅓ in.) long; adult is about 3 mm (⅛ in.) long

WHAT IT LOOKS LIKE: tiny, flat, caterpillarlike larva has a white body and a brown head; adult is a tiny, black, wasplike insect

WHERE YOU FIND IT: within birch leaves

WHEN YOU FIND IT: damage appears from June onward

WHAT IT EATS: larva eats tissue inside birch leaves; adult feeds from flowers

FRIEND OR FOE: foe; makes leaves unsightly

WHAT TO DO: ignore it; keep tree in good shape; parasitic wasps eat larvae

BUG BIO

In May, the adult female sawfly inserts eggs into slits on the upper surface of birch leaves. Larvae hatch and feed inside the leaves for several weeks, a process known as "mining." When sated, larvae drop to the ground and pupate below the soil surface. In two weeks they emerge as adults. There are two or three generations in a summer. Later generations most often feed on tender new leaves. The larval feeding creates brown patches between the leaf surfaces, and if a leaf is held up to the light, larvae can easily be seen. Larvae overwinter in the soil, pupating in spring.

There are two other birch leafminer species with similar characteristics: late birch leafminer (*Heterarthrus nemoratus*), which attacks older leaves, and ambermarked birch leafminer (*Profenusa thomsoni*), which prefers shaded leaves. Both produce only one generation, later in the season.

Miners, like other leaf-eating insects, do not kill trees, so a systemic insecticide, used as a soil drench, should only be used as a last resort. Do not assume it is necessary and do not use it every year. First, evaluate how much leaf surface is missing. Trees can handle a certain reduction in leaf surface area, but insufficient green leaf tissue can result in poor tree health. Parasitic wasps, native or introduced, offer the possibility of control in a very safe manner, but only if no insecticides are used.

Birch trees must be watered well throughout the growing season to remain healthy. They may keep their leaves into late fall and need water until the ground freezes. Often, dead birch treetops are blamed on birch leafminer, when the actual culprit is drought.

Elm leafminer (*Fenusa ulmi*) is similar to birch leafminer. The larva of a slender black sawfly feeds on elm leaves but does little damage. There is only one generation a year. The insects overwinter as pupae in cocoons about 25 mm (1 in.) beneath the soil surface. Systemic insecticides used as a soil drench on birch trees *cannot* be used on elm trees. Keep trees healthy and accept the brown, papery patches on their leaves. The trees don't seem to mind them much.

Poplar leafminer (*Phyllonorycter salicifoliella*) causes similar patches in poplar leaves. The mined areas appear as white ovals on trembling aspen and balsam poplar. Adults lay eggs on the underside of the leaves, and the larvae feed on leaf tissue. The adults are small, brown-and-white moths. They are active for a short time in August, then hibernate in debris on the soil.

Lilac leafminer (*Gracillaria syringella*) damage is caused by the caterpillar of a small, grayish brown moth. Adult females lay eggs on the underside of leaves, and the caterpillars tunnel into and eat leaf tissue. After about three weeks, the caterpillars emerge from the mined area, roll the leaves downward, and feed on them. When they are ready to pupate, they lower themselves to the ground on silken threads and pupate within cocoons in the soil. The moths emerge in early August. There are usually two generations a year; the second generation overwinters as pupae in the soil.

Mining Leaves for a Living

Many insects from different orders make their living mining leaves, producing similar-looking symptoms. These include:

- sawflies (birch leafminer)
- flies, such as lyriomyzid flies (serpentine leafminer)
- moths (lilac leafminer)

For purposes of control, it is useful to know which type is bothering your leaves. For example, BTk, a bacterial control used against caterpillars, could work with a lilac leafminer, but not with a birch leafminer.

Willow redgall sawfly

Pontania proxima

BUG AT A GLANCE (illustration of symptoms, p. 44)
TYPE OF BUG: sawfly
SIZE: larva is 5 mm (⅕ in.) long; adult is about 4 mm (about ⅛ in.) long
WHAT IT LOOKS LIKE: larva is pale green with a black head; adult is a small, slender, black sawfly
WHERE YOU FIND IT: many varieties of willow
WHEN YOU FIND IT: galls appear midsummer
WHAT IT EATS: larva eats willow leaves; adult feeds from flowers
FRIEND OR FOE: benign; a curiosity
WHAT TO DO: think of the galls as leaf decorations

BUG BIO
Slender black sawflies emerge in late spring, mate, and deposit eggs into slits along the midrib of willow leaves. This causes the leaf to create red, oval galls around the eggs, visible on both sides of the leaf. These harmless galls grow as the larvae feed. The first generation pupates under the trees in the summer and the second one overwinters there. Severe infestations can cause premature leaf drop, but most cause cosmetic damage only. The number of galls on a tree may increase with time.

Willow sawfly (*Nematus ventralis*) (p. 122)

Willow sawfly

Nematus ventralis

BUG AT A GLANCE (illustration p. 121)

TYPE OF BUG: sawfly

SIZE: larva is 20 to 24 mm (¾ to 1 in.) long; adult is 8 mm (⅓ in.) long

WHAT IT LOOKS LIKE: larva is black with a distinctive yellow spot on each segment; adult sawfly is an inconspicuous wasplike insect with long antennae

WHERE YOU FIND IT: willow and poplar

WHEN YOU FIND IT: galls appear on leaves in midsummer

WHAT IT EATS: larva eats leaf tissue; adult feeds from flowers

FRIEND OR FOE: benign; a curiosity that does little damage

WHAT TO DO: ignore; use contact insecticide if damage is severe

BUG BIO

In the spring, overwintering male and female adult sawflies emerge from debris or soil beneath willows. Eggs are deposited in slits made in leaves. Larvae mature through five or six instars, eating leaf tissue between leaf veins. Older larvae can eat all but the mid-vein of a leaf. There are two generations each summer. The larvae spin cocoons in the soil or under debris. Adults emerge a week later, in July or August, and the cycle is repeated. They do little damage, as trees can handle quite a few chewed leaves.

Pear sawfly or pear slug

Caliroa cerasi

BUG AT A GLANCE (illustration p. 124)

TYPE OF BUG: sawfly

SIZE: larva is 12 mm (½ in.) long; adult is 5 mm (⅕ in.) long

WHAT IT LOOKS LIKE: larva is shiny and slug shaped; adult is a small, black sawfly

WHERE YOU FIND IT: purpleleaf sand cherry, cotoneaster, hawthorn, pear, plum

WHEN YOU FIND IT: larva first appears in early June, second generation appears in August
WHAT IT EATS: larva eats leaf tissue
FRIEND OR FOE: minor foe; a curiosity that does little damage
WHAT TO DO: a regular blast of cold water from the hose keeps them under control

BUG BIO

Female sawflies insert their eggs into leaves, and the emerging sluglike larvae remove the upper surface of plant tissue, leaving brown areas between the veins. There are two generations on the prairies. The second causes the most damage, as the larvae are more numerous. Larvae overwinter in cocoons below the soil surface and emerge when host plants are in full leaf.

Pear sawflies are often called pear slugs because they look like they could be miniature garden slugs, if garden slugs were black. However, they are no more related to real slugs than you are.

Eriophyid gall mite

Eriophyes spp.

BUG AT A GLANCE (illustration of symptoms, p. 45)

TYPE OF BUG: eriophyid mite
SIZE: 0.2 mm ($\frac{1}{100}$ in.) Long
WHAT IT LOOKS LIKE: tiny, worm-like mite, invisible to the unaided eye
WHERE YOU FIND IT: between the leaf layers of mountain ash trees
WHEN YOU FIND IT: late spring and summer
WHAT IT EATS: sap of mountain ash leaves
FRIEND OR FOE: minor foe
WHAT TO DO: ignore, or let your kids bring the leaves to show-and-tell

BUG BIO

Eriophyid mites are not insects—they are related to spiders and ticks. They are very small—you need a magnifying glass or microscope to see them. They look like tiny worms with only one pair of legs, rather than the usual four. The females overwinter in bark crevices and lay eggs in the spring. There are several generations. As they suck sap from the leaves, their saliva, which contains growth regulators, stimulates the formation of raised, round, white swellings, called galls, on the top surface of otherwise healthy leaves. These raised bumps do little, if any damage. Most of the green tissue is still available for photosynthesis, which is what leaves are for. The galls are used to protect and feed their young. Each gall has a hole in the bottom—an escape hatch on the underside of the leaf.

Similar galls caused by related mites are seen on aspen and black ash. The various eriophyid mites and their lives are not well identified, and there is a lot of research yet to be done to understand them.

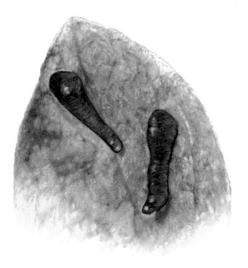

Pear sawfly, pear slug (*Caliroa cerasi*) (p. 122)

Poplar budgall mite

Aceria parapopuli, syn. *Eriophyes parapopuli*

BUG AT A GLANCE (illustration of symptoms, p. 44)

TYPE OF BUG: eriophyid gall mite

SIZE: 0.2 mm (1/100 in.) long

WHAT IT LOOKS LIKE: tiny, slender, round, red creature

WHERE YOU FIND IT: 'Northwest' and other hybrid poplars

WHEN YOU FIND IT: damage first appears in early June; several generations

WHAT IT EATS: buds and new leaves

FRIEND OR FOE: minor foe

WHAT TO DO: remove galls regularly by cutting off affected stems

BUG BIO

The activity of poplar budgall mites feeding on leaf buds stimulates the tree to form swellings that encase the mites. These swellings, called galls, in no way resemble normal growth. They are lumpy, irregular masses of plant tissue that can distort branch growth. All growth stages of mites overwinter together in galls. Adults mate in early spring. Nymphs leave the gall to move to new emerging leaf buds where new galls form. New generations are produced every two to three weeks, all summer long. Wind disperses the tiny mites to new trees. These mites do little damage, but do make trees unsightly. Choose poplars that are less susceptible to this mite.

A similar mite, the ash flower gall mite *(Aceria fraxiniflora),* does its deeds on ash trees.

IO

THE FRUIT FANCIERS

The bugs in this section love the plants you grow for fruit as much as you do. Some like the leaves or roots, and others like the fruit. There are not very many bugs that specialize in making a living from your fruit-bearing plants, perhaps because few fruits will grow on the prairies.

Currant aphid

Cryptomyzus ribis

BUG AT A GLANCE (illustration of symptoms, p. 45)
> **TYPE OF BUG:** aphid
> **SIZE:** 1.2 to 1.8 mm (about ⅟₁₆ in.) long
> **WHAT IT LOOKS LIKE:** pinhead-sized, pale yellow insect with a rounded body; antennae are longer than the body
> **WHERE YOU FIND IT:** all members of currant family
> **WHEN YOU FIND IT:** in late May and June
> **WHAT IT EATS:** sucks sap from underside of leaves
> **FRIEND OR FOE:** minor foe
> **WHAT TO DO:** hose shrubs down frequently with a hard spray of water

BUG BIO
Currant aphids overwinter as eggs that hatch in spring. The nymphs suck sap from the leaf underside, causing puffy, red areas. Generally, these aphids cause little damage. By the time swellings are noticed, the aphids are usually gone. However, if a large enough leaf area is affected, leaves may drop early. Aphids also produce sticky honeydew, which is unsightly.

Currant fruit fly

Epochra canadensis

BUG AT A GLANCE (illustration p. 128)
    TYPE OF BUG: fruit fly
    SIZE: larva is 6 mm (¼ in.) long; adult is 6 to 8 mm (¼ to ⅓ in.) long
    WHAT IT LOOKS LIKE: small, yellowish fly with bands of darker color on the wings; maggot is legless, off-white
    WHERE YOU FIND IT: in fruit of red and white currants and gooseberries
    WHEN YOU FIND IT: maggot damage appears in late July
    WHAT IT EATS: maggot eats currants and gooseberries
    FRIEND OR FOE: foe of fruit growers and fruit eaters
    WHAT TO DO: remove fallen fruit; use a contact insecticide when most of the flower petals have fallen

BUG BIO
Currant fruit flies emerge in late spring, when currants are flowering, and spend some time on the underside of the leaves of the plants. Flies mate and single eggs are laid in growing fruit. The maggots that hatch eat the fruit from the inside and move out after the fruit ripens and falls to the ground. When mature, the maggots pupate in the soil where they remain until spring.

These flies make fruit inedible; no one enjoys wondering if the currant being eaten has a maggot in it. Spraying with insecticides can be effective, but timing is important. Spray flies on leaf undersides in early summer when 80% of the flower petals have fallen but before the fruit is beginning to develop. Repeat in ten days. Choose an insecticide that is safe to use on fruit if you are planning to harvest.

Currant fruit fly larva (*Epochra canadensis*) (p. 127)

Chokecherry midge

Contarinia virginianiae

BUG AT A GLANCE (illustration of symptoms, p. 45)
  TYPE OF BUG: gall midge
  SIZE: adult is 6 mm (¼ in.) long
  WHAT IT LOOKS LIKE: maggot is tiny, orange, and insignificant; adult is a tiny, slim fly
  WHERE YOU FIND IT: inside chokecherries
  WHEN YOU FIND IT: fruit damage appears in June; several generations are produced until late July
  WHAT IT EATS: maggot eats chokecherries
  FRIEND OR FOE: a foe if fruit is wanted
  WHAT TO DO: no known control as maggot cannot be reached in the fruit; break the cycle by disposing of fallen fruit as soon as you see it on the ground

BUG BIO

The damage caused by the chokecherry midge maggot is obvious on chokecherries in late summer. Fruit that would normally be round and deep blue when ripe is pear shaped and yellowish pink. The inside of the fruit is hollow where the maggot has fed. The maggots remain in the fruit until fall when the fruit drops to the ground. The replete maggots crawl from the fallen fruit and overwinter in the soil to pupate, emerging as adults in the spring. If chokecherry trees are kept for ornamental purposes only, then consider the fruit as a protein-enhanced snack for birds.

Strawberry root weevil

Otiorhynchus ovatus

BUG AT A GLANCE
TYPE OF BUG: weevil
SIZE: larva is 12 mm (½ in) long; adult is 6 mm (¼ in.) long
WHAT IT LOOKS LIKE: larva is C-shaped, legless, white and maggot-like, with a well-developed head; adult is a dark brown to black, hard-shelled beetle with the snout typical of weevils
WHERE YOU FIND IT: strawberry, clover, grasses, and weeds
WHEN YOU FIND IT: larva and adult appear in June
WHAT IT EATS: larva eats roots; adult eats leaves and fruit of strawberry plants, weeds, and grasses
FRIEND OR FOE: minor foe; sometimes enters houses
WHAT TO DO: rotate strawberry crops, if possible; use contact insecticide; vacuum indoors; seal window cracks

BUG BIO
Larvae overwinter in the soil and emerge as adults in late spring. The adults crawl along stems, searching for a suitable place to lay eggs. There are no males; the females lay eggs without mating. Eggs for a second generation are laid in late summer; C-shaped, white larvae hatch in two to three weeks and immediately begin feeding on roots. Adults eat strawberry leaves, clover, various grasses, and weeds, and will also feed on strawberries, making small holes in the fruit but doing little damage. In large numbers, they can stunt and distort strawberry plant growth. Seriously affected plants may die.

Contact insecticides can be used on strawberry plants where weevils are present or damage is seen, but read labels carefully to be sure you aren't creating poisonous fruit. A better solution is to rotate crops, but that isn't easy in small city gardens.

Adult strawberry weevils are more often a source of annoyance in homes than in gardens. They enter in the fall during their trek to find a suitable egg-laying site. If your house is in the way, they will go over or through it, crawling on everything. A vacuum cleaner is the best remedy. If you don't want to share your home with weevils, seal cracks along window frames with caulking and install weather stripping under doors.

Raspberry crown borer

Pennisetia marginata

BUG AT A GLANCE (illustration p. 132)

TYPE OF BUG: clearwing moth

SIZE: caterpillar is 25 mm (1 in.) long; adult wingspan is 25 to 30 mm (1 to 1¼ in.)

WHAT IT LOOKS LIKE: caterpillar is white with a dark head; adult moth resembles a yellowjacket wasp

WHERE YOU FIND IT: raspberry canes

WHEN YOU FIND IT: damage appears in June on new and old canes

WHAT IT EATS: caterpillar eats new raspberry canes; adult sips nectar

FRIEND OR FOE: foe; weakens raspberry canes

WHAT TO DO: remove old canes to break the cycle; use chemical soil drench or spray lower canes if problem is severe

BUG BIO

In late summer, raspberry crown borers lay eggs on the underside of raspberry leaves. Caterpillars emerge in October and overwinter at the base of raspberry plants in separate cells. In spring, the caterpillars burrow into the base of canes, causing swellings (galls) at, or just beneath, ground level. In the second season, they overwinter inside canes and emerge the following spring. Mature caterpillars pupate in midsummer under the cane bark near the ground. Moths emerge in the fall.

Caterpillar feeding weakens the canes, causing leaf wilt. Remove old canes that have galls at their bases in the spring and fall to break the cycle. Insecticides aren't usually necessary except in commercial plantings.

Imported currantworm

Nematus ribesii

BUG AT A GLANCE (illustration p. 132)

TYPE OF BUG: sawfly

SIZE: mature larva is 20 mm (¾ in.) long; adult is 8 mm (⅓ in.) long

WHAT IT LOOKS LIKE: young larva is pale green with a black head and spots; mature larva is green with a pale yellow head; adult sawfly is black with pale lines on the abdomen

WHERE YOU FIND IT: under leaves of red and white currants and gooseberries

WHEN YOU FIND IT: first generation appears in June, second generation in July

WHAT IT EATS: larva eats leaves of all currants, except black currants

FRIEND OR FOE: a nasty foe

WHAT TO DO: handpick; spray water at it with a well-aimed hose; use contact insecticides when larvae are visible

BUG BIO

Larvae or pupae of imported currantworms overwinter in cocoons in the soil. Adult sawflies emerge in early summer. Eggs are laid under currant leaves. The voracious little larvae that emerge waste no time munching away the currant leaves. After two to three weeks, they pupate in the soil. There are two generations a year.

The larvae are difficult to see because they are often on the inside of the bush, under the leaves. Large numbers of larvae can defoliate a shrub very quickly. Often the first thing a dismayed gardener notices is a shrub without leaves.

Raspberry crown borer (*Pennisetia marginata*) (p. 130)

Imported currantworm (*Nematus ribesii*) (p. 131)

II

THE GROUND DWELLERS

There is a myriad of critters at work in our soil and amongst the leaf litter in our gardens. We rarely notice them and in most cases they are helping gardeners by eating potential pests, and aerating and improving the soil.

Junebug or May beetle

Phyllophaga spp.

BUG AT A GLANCE

TYPE OF BUG: scarab beetle

SIZE: grub is 25 to 30 mm (1 to 1¼ in.) long; adult beetle is up to 25 mm (1 in.) long

WHAT IT LOOKS LIKE: grub is white and C-shaped; adult is a shiny, dark, reddish or brown beetle with obvious antennae

WHERE YOU FIND IT: grub lives underground within the root zone of turf and other grasses; adult emerges from underground at night and is attracted by light

WHEN YOU FIND IT: adult eats leaves in June; larval damage to roots appears in July and August

WHAT IT EATS: grub eats the roots of turf and other grasses; adult eats leaves

FRIEND OR FOE: minor foe

WHAT TO DO: keep your lawn healthy and you won't mind sharing a few roots

BUG BIO

Adults emerge in spring, mate, and lay eggs underground. The white, C-shaped grubs emerge in a few weeks, remaining underground. They burrow deeply in the fall and then return to shallower depths to feed in spring. They pupate in the second summer and emerge shortly thereafter as adults, but remain underground until their third year. Junebug grubs are distinguished from other white grubs by the presence of a double row of tiny spines on the underside of the last body segment.

Sometimes Junebugs are known as May beetles. These common names, given because of the time of year when the beetles are seen, can be misleading. A beetle seen in May in one region might be seen in June in another.

Dung beetles and tumblebugs, a group of scarab beetles related to the June bug, have the fascinating habit of forming spherical balls of dung. These beautifully crafted balls are rolled to a previously excavated pit. The female then deposits an egg in the ball and buries it, all for the benefit of the baby dung beetle, which eats the dung when it hatches. Some species make their home on the prairies, but you won't spot them in your garden unless you keep cattle there.

Sacred Scarabs

To ancient Egyptians, the appearance of the scarab beetle (*Scarabaeus sacer*) rolling a ball of dung across the mud flats of the Nile was identified with the rolling of the sun across the sky by the great sun god Ra. Thus, these beetles became sacred symbols in Egypt. Scarab amulets were popular and important symbols for rich and poor alike.

European ground beetle, purple-rimmed carabus

Carabus nemoralis

BUG AT A GLANCE (illustration p. 136)

    TYPE OF BUG: carabid beetle

    SIZE: can be over 20 mm (¾ in.) long

    WHAT IT LOOKS LIKE: shiny, black beetle with longitudinal ridges or bumps on the elytra; purple edging on the elytra

    WHERE YOU FIND IT: under stones, boards, and logs in moist areas

    WHEN YOU FIND IT: active at night; most commonly observed in late summer

    WHAT IT EATS: other insects

    FRIEND OR FOE: a good friend

    WHAT TO DO: don't scream; carefully replace the rock you just picked up

BUG BIO

Female European ground beetles lay eggs in the soil; the emerging grubs feed in the soil or on it, under debris. Depending on the species or region, there may be more than one generation per year. The larvae overwinter in soil. The larvae and adults are voracious consumers of insects.

Several other species of ground beetles may be found scurrying around in the leaf litter of your garden. The common ground beetle (*Pterostychus melanarius*) resembles the European ground beetle without the purple rim, and the elytra have regular, longitudinal grooves. It also consumes vast quantities of insects. Both the common ground beetle and the European ground beetle are introduced species. Although introduced species can be detrimental, so far these beetles have been well behaved and do not seem to have had a negative effect on native carabids. Related native beetles called fiery hunters (*Calosoma* spp.) actively pursue caterpillars in trees. These beetles have bright spots on their elytra.

Ground beetles sometimes cause panic when found indoors. They enter through cracks around doors, windows, and foundations, in search of insect food. They do not survive for long indoors and can be eliminated by sweeping and vacuuming.

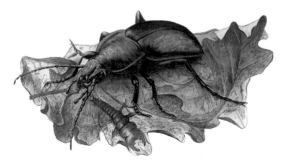

European ground beetle (*Carabus nemoralis*) (p. 135)

Rove beetle

Family Staphylinidae

BUG AT A GLANCE

TYPE OF BUG: rove beetle

SIZE: some species are up to 20 mm (¾ in.) long

WHAT IT LOOKS LIKE: a long, narrow-bodied beetle, with short elytra and a visible abdomen; often hairy

WHERE YOU FIND IT: in the ground, under leaf litter and stones, in ant nests

WHEN YOU FIND IT: spring to fall; active at night

WHAT IT EATS: grubs, maggots, live or dead ants, and aphids

FRIEND OR FOE: rarely noticed friend

WHAT TO DO: let it do what it does best; avoid soil pesticides

BUG BIO

Rove beetles are fast-moving, narrow beetles that attack insects, grubs, and root maggots in the soil. They look somewhat like earwigs without pincers. Rove beetles are unusual in that their elytra are short and do not cover the entire abdomen. They are able to fold their long wings intricately under these short elytra. Surpisingly, rove beetles can fly quite well.

Occasionally, these super-efficient rove beetles will climb up plants at night to eat aphids. Talk about good service!

Sod webworm

Family Pyralidae
Subfamily Crambinae

BUG AT A GLANCE

TYPE OF BUG: grass moth caterpillar
SIZE: caterpillar is up to 20 mm (¾ in.) long; adult
wingspan is 12 to 39 mm (½ to 1½ in.)
WHAT IT LOOKS LIKE: caterpillar is tan with dark spots
and has a dark-colored head; adult is a small, white moth
WHERE YOU FIND IT: caterpillar is found in soil where
there is, or was, grass; adult rests amongst blades of
grass and is attracted to lights at night
WHEN YOU FIND IT: caterpillar damage to lawns
appears from July to September
WHAT IT EATS: larva eats grass roots; adults do not feed
FRIEND OR FOE: potentially serious foe
WHAT TO DO: keep your lawn healthy; use BTk on severe
infestations; ground and rove beetles can control them

BUG BIO

Caterpillars that have overwintered feed for a short time in spring, then
pupate in the soil, giving rise to adults in summer. Adults fly from dusk
to dawn and rest during the day. They scatter their eggs amongst grasses
and the eggs hatch in a week. The caterpillars live in tunnels lined with
silk webbing, in the thatch or just below the surface of the soil, emerging
from their tunnels to chew grass blades at night. There are usually two or
three generations per year, depending on the species and the region.

Grass moths are the small, papery moths that fly up when you mow
the lawn. They have unusual mouthparts that give them the appearance
of having snouts. They fold their wings around their bodies when resting.
The presence of a few moths is not necessarily cause for alarm.

The first signs of a problem are patches of dead grass in an otherwise
healthy lawn, usually a sunny, dry lawn rather than a shaded or moist lawn.
The telltale webbing may also be observed if you dig below the surface of
the ground. Damage is patchy at first but can eventually become extensive.

Healthy lawns are less vulnerable to an attack by sod webworms.
Water your lawn well and not too often, and maintain grass blade
height at about 5 cm (2 in.). Use BTk, a bacterial insecticide that kills

only caterpillars (the larvae of moths and butterflies), if an infestation is serious.

Another member of the Pyralidae, the European corn borer (*Ostrinia nubilalis*), is only a problem if you grow corn. The corn borer is in the same family as the sod webworm because corn is, in fact, nothing more than a very tall grass.

Glassy cutworm

Family Noctuidae
Apamea devastator, syn. *Crymodes devastator*

BUG AT A GLANCE (illustration p. 141)

TYPE OF BUG: noctuid moth caterpillar

SIZE: mature caterpillar is 35 to 40 mm (1⅜ to 1½ in.) long; adult wingspan is 40 to 45 mm (1½ to 1¾ in.)

WHAT IT LOOKS LIKE: caterpillar is translucent, short, fat, greenish gray, with a dark head; adult moth is grayish with dark markings on fore wings

WHERE YOU FIND IT: garden soil

WHEN YOU FIND IT: plant damage appears from July to September

WHAT IT EATS: caterpillar eats grass, cereal crops, corn, and vegetables

FRIEND OR FOE: foe

WHAT TO DO: put collars around stems of susceptible plants; use insecticidal dusts if infestation is severe

BUG BIO

The young caterpillars overwinter underground. They resume feeding in spring when new plant growth is available and pupate in soil by the end of June. Adults emerge in July and can be seen until early September. The female moths lay eggs at the base of host plants. There is only one generation per year.

The caterpillars chew off grass blades at ground level and pull them down into the soil, leaving patches of dead grass. They will also feed on corn, other vegetables, and cereal crops planted where grass previously grew.

Another species found on the prairies is the army cutworm (*Euxoa auxiliaris*). These cutworms emerge from soil at night and eat the leaves of cereal and vegetable crops. The adult moths appear briefly in June to feed and then go dormant through most of the summer, often in buildings.

Army cutworms tend to appear in large numbers during an outbreak year, which occurs following a year with an abnormally dry summer and a wet autumn.

The redbacked cutworm (*Euxoa ochrogaster*) has similarly nasty habits. This dull gray caterpillar has a reddish stripe down the back. Although an important agricultural pest, it may also fell seedlings of a number of garden plants, from late May through late July. The redbacked cutworm lays its eggs in the fall, in light, dry soil.

The medium-sized adult moths of cutworms, especially of the army cutworm, are usually called miller moths, because their delicate wing scales are easily rubbed off and reminded early settlers of flour. They are moths you often find flapping around inside your home in late summer. They do not lay eggs or do any damage indoors, and no, they don't eat your clothes. The moths responsible for aerating your fine woolens are members of the Tineid or clothes moth family.

Ant

Family Formicidae

BUG AT A GLANCE
TYPE OF BUG: ant
SIZE: 4 to 13 mm (⅛ to ½ in.) long
WHAT IT LOOKS LIKE: usually a wingless, shiny black or reddish insect with three distinct body parts and "elbowed" antennae
WHERE YOU FIND IT: everywhere there is suitable food and a place for an underground nest
WHEN YOU FIND IT: spring to fall
WHAT IT EATS: larva feeds on insects or vegetable matter brought by adults; adult eats insects, small spiders, nectar, sap, or vegetable matter, depending on the species
FRIEND OR FOE: usually benign; sometimes disrupts roots; may ruin the appearance of a lawn; rarely chews plants
WHAT TO DO: usually nothing; persistently disturb problem nests using a stick, shovel, or boiling water

BUG BIO
If ants—amongst the most fascinating of the planet's creatures—could read, they would be proud that there is a Pulitzer prize-winning book

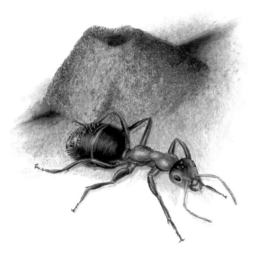

Ant (Family Formicidae)

devoted entirely to their kind. *The Ants*, by ethnobiologists Edward O. Wilson and Bert Holldöbler, is revered by all serious natural history afficionados. An entirely new discipline, the science of sociobiology, was launched by Wilson largely as the result of a lifetime of studying ants.

All species of ants live in colonies. Colonies may be large or small, and colonial behaviors can vary tremendously between the species. In some species there may be several castes of ants, all varying in size and detail. Ants perform colony tasks according to their caste. For example, large soldier ants of some species guard the nest entrances and may use their own heads as doors.

Sterile workers care for the eggs, larvae, and pupae in the colonial nest. One or more queens in a nest lay all of the fertile eggs. In some species the workers can lay sterile "food" eggs. Once a year, winged males and females swarm from the nest and mate in mid-air. Successfully mated females begin new colonies; the males and unsuccessful females die. The original colony continues and may persist for many years.

In the tropics, ants may constitute the largest biomass of all subterranean organisms. In our northerly climate, the number and diversity of ants are comparatively sparse, but ants may still be important soil-turners and aerators, second only to earthworms.

If ants are not disrupting or otherwise interfering with your plants, they are best left alone. Many species are predators of other, perhaps unwanted, insects. Ants are also important soil aerators. If ants get into your house, find and block points of access and clean the area that they were traveling through. If you must get rid of an ant nest, disrupt it with a shovel or heavy watering a few times to convince them to leave.

The groups of ants that are of interest to the prairie gardener are: wood ants (*Formica* spp.), carpenter ants (*Camponotus* spp.), and harvester ants (*Pogonomymex* spp.).

Wood ants (*Formica* spp.) The small black or red ants scurrying around your patio might include species of wood ants. Although on the small side (4 to 8 mm, ⅛ to ⅓ in.), wood ants are fierce, at least towards other insects, because they are predators and scavengers. You may spot them hauling live or dead insect prey to their nests. They do not sting, but do have a fierce bite and can spray formic acid from the abdomen to enhance inflicted pain.

Wood ants may make slaves of other ants. From time to time they raid colonies of the same or different species and make off with pupae from the invaded nest. They raise these pupae as their own, and the adults that hatch go about their lives in their new colony, none the wiser.

Wood ants are amongst the ants that tend and herd aphids. The aphids receive protection from predators, and in return, the ants eat the honeydew that the aphids continuously exude. Ants love honeydew the way some people love chocolate—they can't resist it.

Carpenter ants (*Camponotus* spp.) Carpenter ants are large, black ants that can be over 12 mm (½ in.) long. Despite their size, they are not very aggressive; their strong jaws are used for chewing wood. Carpenter ants make their nests in wood that has already begun to rot, and not in healthy trees, or in sound wooden structures. However, their excavations may further weaken an already weak tree or compromise a rotting building structure. These ants do not eat the wood, but instead remove it to make the passageways and chambers of their nests. Piles of sawdust outside nest openings are a sign that they are present.

If you discover carpenter ant excavations in one of your trees, thank the ants for pointing out its poor health. If the tree has a lot of rotten wood, it may need to be removed for safety reasons. If it can be salvaged, determine the nature of the problem causing the rot and take the appropriate steps. Consult a reputable arborist.

Harvester ants (*Pogonomyrmex* spp.) Harvester ants are true

Glassy cutworm (*Apamea devastator*, syn. *Crymodes devastator*) (p. 138)

denizens of the western prairies. All species except one are found west of the Mississippi River. They are about 13 mm (½ in.) long, are reddish brown to black in color, and have a somewhat squarish head.

These ants build conspicuously mounded nests incorporating fine, dried plant debris, stones, and other available tidbits. The specially chosen objects covering a mound are believed to act as a thermal energy collector to keep the temperature inside the nest warm. This penchant for covering nest mounds with small objects sometimes benefits archaeologists seeking small artifacts. These ants also clear away the vegetation inside a wide perimeter around their nests. Colonies may be very long-lived, but it is not unusual for them to relocate if they no longer like the current nest site. As their name suggests, harvester ants collect seeds for food. They may also make an occasional meal of another insect.

Harvester ants may pose a problem if their nests become large in inconvenient areas, such as lawns. These ants also have an exceedingly painful and toxic sting, so it is wise to remove nests from areas where children or pets play.

Millipede

Class Diplopoda
Order Juliidae

BUG AT A GLANCE (illustration p. 144)
TYPE OF BUG: millipede
SIZE: less than 40 mm (1½ in.) long
WHAT IT LOOKS LIKE: dark, shiny, tubular arthropod with many segments and two pairs of legs per segment; often found curled up
WHERE YOU FIND IT: in dark, dampish areas with ample decaying vegetation
WHEN YOU FIND IT: spring to fall; active at night
WHAT IT EATS: decaying vegetation; the small greenhouse millipede (*Oxidus gracilis*) is sometimes blamed inconclusively for chewing on greenhouse plants
FRIEND OR FOE: friend; millipedes are vegetation recyclers
WHAT TO DO: let it get its rest

BUG BIO
Millipedes are sometimes confused with centipedes or even worms. Their

jointed legs and hard exoskeleton reveal them to be arthropods. Their bodies are tubular, composed of many short segments, and their myriad legs are arranged neatly under the body, two pairs to a segment. A pair of short-segmented antennae is found at the front end. In tropical countries, millipede species may be over 30 cm (12 in.) long, but squeamish gardeners will be glad that prairie millipedes seldom exceed a few centimeters (about 1 in.) in length.

Millipedes are benign, plodding creatures; when threatened, they often coil up. Most creatures looking to them for a meal learn quickly that millipedes are not tasty and may in fact be noxious. Some millipedes can emit a cyanide-containing gas from holes in their sides if they really need to press a point. They are harmless to people.

Centipede

Class Chilopoda
Lithobius spp.

BUG AT A GLANCE
TYPE OF BUG: centipede
SIZE: 20 to 40 mm (¾ to 1½ in.) long
WHAT IT LOOKS LIKE: flattened, multi-legged creature with long legs splayed to the side; usually a rusty orange color
WHERE YOU FIND IT: in dark, dampish places, including basements
WHEN YOU FIND IT: spring to fall; active at night
WHAT IT EATS: any small creatures it can run down and subdue
FRIEND OR FOE: friend and ally
WHAT TO DO: let it get on with its life

BUG BIO
You may immediately distrust centipedes because of their long snaky appearance, which is made more sinister by long, rapidly scurrying legs, and because you may have found them in your home. In fact, centipedes are voracious predators of other, more slowly moving arthropods, such as beetles.

Centipedes can be distinguished from millipedes by their flattened bodies, long splayed legs, and rapid movement. They have one pair of legs per body segment. A pair of venomous fangs found at the front end is used to suppress prey much as a spider does. Thankfully, prairie

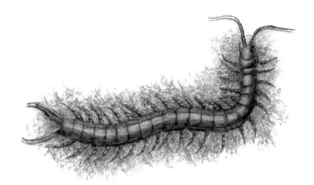

Centipede (*Lithobius* spp.)

centipedes are fairly small and not a menace to people.

If you find centipedes in your basement and don't care to share your home with them, remove the damp, dark conditions that they enjoy. Also eliminate conditions that provide a home to whatever creatures they feast upon.

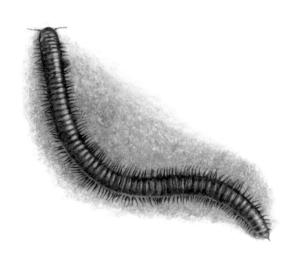

Millipede (Class Diplopoda) (p. 142)

Symphylan

Class Symphyla
Scutigerella immaculata

BUG AT A GLANCE (no illustration)
    TYPE OF BUG: small, vaguely centipedelike arthropod
    SIZE: 3 to 6 mm (⅛ to ¼ in.) long
    WHAT IT LOOKS LIKE: very small, pale, flattened arthropod with twelve pairs of legs when mature and long, many-segmented antennae
    WHERE YOU FIND IT: in moist, humus-rich, preferably sandy soil
    WHEN YOU FIND IT: damage becomes obvious as summer progresses, they are not seen aboveground
    WHAT IT EATS: roots of certain plants
    FRIEND OR FOE: minor foe
    WHAT TO DO: nothing, prairie gardeners have little to worry about

BUG BIO
Symphylans are sometimes called "garden centipedes," but they are not centipedes. In any case, the name "garden centipede" might imply that they are "good" bugs, when, in fact, symphylans can be a major agricultural pest of some commercial crops, such as asparagus, mint, and other vegetables, mainly on the west coast. They are not a problem for prairie gardeners, however. These arthropods are difficult to spot because they quickly run away from light.

Wolf Spider

Family Lycosidae

BUG AT A GLANCE
TYPE OF BUG: wolf spider
SIZE: 3 to 35 mm (⅛ to 1⅜ in.) long, depending on the species
WHAT IT LOOKS LIKE: long-legged spider, somewhat hairy, often gray or brown
WHERE YOU FIND IT: on the ground

WHEN YOU FIND IT: adults most commonly observed in summer
WHAT IT EATS: insects and other small organisms
FRIEND OR FOE: always a gardener's friend
WHAT TO DO: don't step on it

BUG BIO

Wolf spiders are hunting spiders that have forsaken catching meals in webs for running them down on the ground. They also have fairly good eyesight for spiders, which they need to spot a potential meal from a few centimeters (about an inch) away. Although they don't spin webs, they may use silk to line burrows and to make an egg sac.

A female wolf spider is a very protective mother. She carefully encases her eggs in a tough silken egg sac, which she attaches to her spinnerets and drags around with her. This gives her the appearance, at first, of having an extra white or bluish abdomen. Although a wolf spider mother will fiercely resist efforts to have her egg case taken away, experiments have shown that, no matter how diligent, she is easily fooled into accepting a replacement egg case, for example, a ball of cork roughly the same size as her egg sac.

At the correct time, the mother opens her egg sac to let the hatched spiderlings out, something they seem unable to do for themselves. Then, amazingly, all of them immediately hop onto their mother's back where they remain for a week or so. They do not eat during this interval, but do drink any water that accumulates on the mother's back. If they fall off, they must quickly get back on or be left behind. At some point, they leave their mother en masse and embark on their separate lives.

Sowbug

Class Crustacea
Order Isopoda

BUG AT A GLANCE (illustration p. 148)

TYPE OF BUG: terrestrial crustacean
SIZE: up to 15 mm (⅝ in.) long
WHAT IT LOOKS LIKE: gray, multi-legged creature with an elliptical body, two pairs of short antennae, seven pairs of legs, and a pair of tail-like appendages
WHERE YOU FIND IT: dark, very moist places

WHEN YOU FIND IT: spring to fall
WHAT IT EATS: decaying vegetable or animal matter, rarely living plants
FRIEND OR FOE: benign; not usually a problem for gardeners
WHAT TO DO: eliminate it from your list of worries

BUG BIO

Sowbugs are relatives of crabs and lobsters. They are amongst the very few crustaceans living a terrestrial life and must have permanently moist surroundings to thrive. Sowbugs are also known as "wood lice." A related creature, the pillbug, is very similar, except that pillbugs can roll into a ball, which sowbugs cannot do. Pillbugs also lack the tail-like appendages of a sowbug.

Earthworm

Phylum Annelida
Class Oligochaeta
Family Lumbricidae

BUG AT A GLANCE

TYPE OF BUG: lumbricid worm
SIZE: up to 30 cm (12 in.) long for the large dew worms
WHAT IT LOOKS LIKE: from a large "dew worm" to smaller, reddish species; legless, moist, tubular, pink to dark red in color
WHERE YOU FIND IT: everywhere in your soil, if you are lucky
WHEN YOU FIND IT: spring to fall, after ground has thawed
WHAT IT EATS: various amounts of decomposing vegetation and soil depending on the species
FRIEND OR FOE: there is no truer friend of the soil
WHAT TO DO: let it fulfill its wormy life; break up clods of clay on the lawn with gypsum

BUG BIO

You likely know that earthworms are beneficial because they eat decaying vegetation, hastening the transformation of plant material into new plant nutrients. Earthworms also improve soil texture and aeration through their movements. The large dew worms may bring clay to the surface during their excavations, which becomes lumpy and hard underfoot, but they are still aerating your lawn and dragging important humus to the root zone of the grass. It is very bad practice to kill them, as this cannot be accomplished without killing other worms.

What a sorry state soil would be in if there were no worms. In fact, the earliest explorers of the prairies would not have found any worms here. Earthworms became extinct wherever

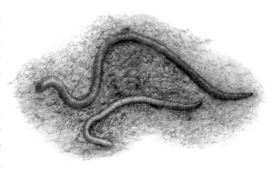

Earthworm (Family Lumbricidae)

glaciation occurred, and the entire prairie region was glaciated many times, the last glaciers retreating to their current remnants in the mountains about 10,000 years ago. Eventually, earthworms from unglaciated areas re-populate these areas, but this natural process takes a very long time. Unwittingly, and to our benefit today, earthworms were re-introduced as humans began to settle westward, so prairie worms are exotic species, either from Europe, Asia, or more southerly areas of North America. Although very often the introduction of foreign species turns out to be detrimental, the prairies have been well served.

Earthworms are hermaphroditic. Every worm is both male and female, but still must mate to reproduce. Each mated worm produces an egg sac from which new worms eventually emerge.

Unlike arthropods, worms have no skeletons and simply grow larger as they get older. All earthworms eat decaying organic matter as well as amounts of soil, depending on the species. Some construct vertical burrows; others move through shallow, horizontal burrows.

There are about a dozen species of earthworms on the prairies. Keeners can even determine the species by looking at details of the clitellum, which is the pronounced "collar" that all mature earthworms have.

If the clay-rich lumps left by large worms bother you, sprinkle gypsum on the lumps, water them, and then rake them out smooth when the soil is dry.

Sowbug (Order Isopoda)
(p. 146)

slug

Phylum Mollusca
Class Gastropoda
Order Stylommatophora

BUG AT A GLANCE
TYPE OF BUG: slug
SIZE: up to 25 mm (1 in.) long, stretched out
WHAT IT LOOKS LIKE: beige or grayish, soft-bodied creature with two tentacles
WHERE YOU FIND IT: under rocks, boards, or heavy mulch in moist areas by day; on plants at night
WHEN YOU FIND IT: active at night; becomes more numerous as summer progresses
WHAT IT EATS: your juiciest and most choice plants
FRIEND OR FOE: a definite foe
WHAT TO DO: remove potential hiding places from the garden; handpick late in the evening or early morning; spread diatomaceous earth around susceptible plants; apply physical barriers; use slug bait

BUG BIO

Slugs are snails without shells. Actually, slugs do have vestiges of a shell but they are tucked away within the body. The slugs most likely to be a problem in prairie gardens are introduced species from Europe. They are small—no more than a few centimeters (about an inch) long when stretched out.

Slugs move about on a muscular foot over a sheet of slime, which they secrete to help them glide. The silvery trails of dried slug slime that remain on plants and pathways after slugs have passed through are familiar sights in the garden.

A slug's head is relatively well defined and characterized by a pair of tentacles bearing eyes. Slugs use their small rasping mouthparts, called radulae, to grind away at the soft tissues of plants, leaving large, irregular telltale holes in the foliage. They come out at night to feed and hide under rocks, boards, or thick mulch in the daytime.

Slugs are hermaphroditic, with each individual containing both male and female reproductive parts. However, they must mate with another slug to produce eggs. Slugs lay their jellylike egg masses in moist crevices.

Birds, such as the magpies that visit your garden early in the morning, consider slugs a nutritious morsel, but there is nothing lovely about slugs for gardeners, who have come up with many strategies for defeating them. The cheapest and most time-consuming method is to go out at night and handpick them, wearing gloves or using tweezers. Success is limited only by your diligence.

Commercial slug baits are very effective. In the past, available slug baits were also toxic to other animals and people, but those recently introduced into the market are much safer. This is the best course of action for treating a persistent slug problem.

Wily gardeners use homemade baits with some success. A half grapefruit rind placed domelike on the ground rounds up slugs overnight. Slugs hide underneath the grapefruit and can be dispatched in the morning. Some people put shallow pans of beer out to attract and drown them, but some slugs seem capable of drinking the beer and then leaving again to commit more mayhem.

Physical barriers such as copper collars are also effective slug controls, as long as they completely encircle each plant requiring protection. A sprinkling of diatomaceous earth around susceptible plants works temporarily, but must be re-applied after rain or hand watering. Diatomaceous earth consists of the ground-up, glassy shells of small marine plankton called diatoms. Essentially fine glass, it shreds the body of any slug that attempts to crawl over it.

12

THE PERENNIAL PROWLERS

You could find bugs in this section almost anywhere in your garden where there are plants to eat or prey to catch. You might spot them along the foundations of your house, on your windowsills and fences, or anywhere at all that might be "bug-friendly."

Short-horned grasshopper

Family Acrididae

BUG AT A GLANCE

TYPE OF BUG: short-horned grasshopper
SIZE: usually 15 to 50 mm (⅝ to 2 in.) long when mature
WHAT IT LOOKS LIKE: a long-bodied insect with long hind legs, a distinctive head, prominent eyes, and antennae shorter than the body length; often shows brightly colored wings when flying
WHERE YOU FIND IT: a variety of habitats, commonly in grassy meadows
WHEN YOU FIND IT: spring to fall; becomes especially numerous in summer
WHAT IT EATS: a wide variety of plants
FRIEND OR FOE: usually benign; some species are a potential foe if present in large numbers
WHAT TO DO: for best results, use pesticides when grasshoppers are small; blister beetle larvae eat grasshopper eggs; guinea hens and other poultry eat grasshoppers

BUG BIO

In late summer it is impossible to walk anywhere through prairie grassland without sending grasshoppers flying in every direction. Grasshoppers are almost synonymous with the prairies. Although some are significant crop pests, grasshoppers as a whole are important members of a healthy prairie ecosystem and are generally not a problem in gardens.

Grasshoppers undergo gradual metamorphosis. Eggs are laid in the ground or inside plant tissue in the fall. In the spring, the newly hatched grasshoppers resemble tiny, wingless versions of adults. Some species overwinter as juveniles. Grasshoppers molt several times, becoming larger and more adultlike each time. The final molt produces the winged adult. Like birds, grasshoppers are said to have fledged. For most species there is only one generation each year.

Grasshoppers "sing" by rubbing a pegged leg against a front wing, referred to as stridulation; this process can be crudely simulated by rubbing a thumbnail along the teeth of a comb. Their songs are characteristic for their species. In most cases, the males serenade the females. Grasshoppers have hearing organs on the base of the abdomen, rather than ears, to hear this love song.

The early-season grasshoppers, which have overwintered as juveniles, are not pest species and are an important source of food for birds. Don't worry if you see these grasshoppers and don't kill them. Use the following rules of thumb to learn to tell potentially harmful species from others:

• grasshoppers flying in April and May are non-pest species

• grasshoppers with club-ended antennae are not to be feared

• species showing red, orange, or yellow wings in flight are not pests (from D. L. Johnson's *Grasshoppers* web site, see references p. 191)

The red-shanked grasshopper (*Xanthippus corallipes latefasciatus*) is an abundant and attractive non-pest species that may be seen in rural areas early in the spring. This large, lumpy grasshopper has reddish orange hind legs.

Agricultural pests include several species of *Melanoplus*, such as the two-striped grasshopper (*M. bivittatus*) (illustrated). However, the presence of agricultural pest species in your garden is not necessarily cause for concern, as there is evidence that some chewing may actually stimulate plant growth. Grasshoppers do not carry any plant or animal disease, and although their eggs are laid in the ground, they do not harm plant roots. (Dan Johnson, Lethbridge Research Centre, Agriculture and Agri-food Canada, personal communication.)

Gardeners living in areas where grasshopper outbreaks are known to occur may have more cause for concern. Prepare yourself by finding out as early as you can if an outbreak is expected in your area. Various chemical controls and poisoned baits are most effective when grasshoppers are small. If you live in a rural area, you may be able to keep guinea hens or other poultry, which help keep grasshopper numbers down.

Large numbers of grasshoppers can defoliate almost everything in a garden. If you are caught in a full-blown attack of mature grasshoppers, protect your most cherished shrubs or plants by covering them with sturdy window screening or other tough, fine mesh. Trees and shrubs in good condition are likely to survive an attack. It may be of some comfort to know that the grasshopper feces left behind are a clean and rich source of nitrogen (Dan Johnson, Lethbridge Research Centre, Agriculture and Agri-food Canada, personal communication). Often, what seems out of control and devastating is just part of the larger cycle of life, death, and rebirth.

Although most grasshopper species on the northern prairies are the short-horned grasshoppers, another family—the long-horned grasshoppers and katydids (Family Tettigoniidae)—is also represented by a few species, including Mormon crickets (*Anabrus simplex*) and a few katydids. Long-horned grasshoppers have antennae longer than their bodies, whereas short-horned grasshoppers' antennae are shorter than their bodies. The long-horned grasshoppers stridulate by rubbing their fore wings together and have their hearing organs on their front legs.

A Swarm of Locusts

When certain species of short-horned grasshoppers swarm, they are sometimes referred to as locusts. Real locusts are an Old World phenomenon and are like something out of a science fiction movie, acting out relatively benign lives until something triggers a generation to develop traits associated with swarming, such as longer wings, brighter coloration, and an insatiable appetite. These "shape shifters" can devastate huge areas of cropland when they get into the migratory mode.

There are no longer any grasshoppers that act this way on the northern plains. However, in the nineteenth century migratory swarms of the Rocky Mountain grasshopper (*Caloptenus spretus*) blackened the sun, caused train wheels to slip on the tracks, and clogged up sewers when it rained. Curiously, these grasshoppers appear to be extinct, or else they lead more discreet lives. Because the economic devastation can be so profound, a lot of research has been done to determine why some grasshoppers suddenly become gregarious and occur in such prodigious numbers.

Crickets

Family Gryllidae
Subfamily Gryllinae (includes field crickets)
Subfamily Oecanthinae (tree crickets)

BUG AT A GLANCE

TYPE OF BUG: cricket

SIZE: 20 to 25 mm (¾ to 1 in.) long

WHAT THEY LOOK LIKE: field cricket is reddish brown to black; tree cricket is a light green, oblong shape with long antennae and large, slightly splayed hind legs

WHERE YOU FIND THEM: a variety of habitats; commonly in grassy meadows

WHEN YOU FIND THEM: summer; active at night

WHAT THEY EAT: most are omnivorous or herbivorous; tree cricket relishes soft-bodied insects such as aphids

FRIEND OR FOE: benign; may become a household pest

WHAT TO DO: relax and enjoy their pleasant songs on warm summer evenings

BUG BIO

Like grasshoppers, crickets undergo gradual metamorphosis. Eggs are laid in the ground or inside plant stems in late summer or early fall, where they overwinter. The juvenile crickets molt many times before becoming full-fledged adults. Unlike the rasping call of grasshoppers, cricket calls have a pleasant musical pitch. Crickets are divided into several subfamilies, including tree crickets, ground crickets, and field crickets. Crickets most commonly seen on the prairies include the black fall field cricket (*Gryllus pennsylvanicus*) and the similar spring field cricket (*G. veletis*).

One Person's Music ...

... is another person's noise. Crickets are not generally considered to be pests, but in this case, it is all in the ear of the listener. Whereas the common house cricket (*Acheta domesticus*) is sometimes considered a pest in North American households because of its incessant chirping, it has long been a tradition in Asian households to keep caged crickets for their melodious song.

Minute pirate bug

Orius tristicolor and other species

BUG AT A GLANCE (no illustration)
>   **TYPE OF BUG:** anthocorid bug
>   **SIZE:** 2 to 5 mm ($\frac{1}{10}$ to $\frac{1}{5}$ in.) long
>   **WHAT IT LOOKS LIKE:** tiny, oval, and flat with a pointed head; dark, with whitish wing markings
>   **WHERE YOU FIND IT:** flowers, leaf litter, or bark
>   **WHEN YOU FIND IT:** summer; several generations
>   **WHAT IT EATS:** nymph eats small insects; adult eats spider mites, thrips, aphids, and the crawler stage of scale
>   **FRIEND OR FOE:** an aphid-eating friend
>   **WHAT TO DO:** appreciate its value

BUG BIO

There are many species of these tiny bugs in North America, all of which are "good," although they can deliver a painful, but not poisonous, bite if handled.

After mating in early spring, females lay eggs in plant tissue. There are several generations in a summer. When the day length is short enough, the last adult generation becomes inactive and beds down in leaf litter to overwinter.

Pirate bugs feed on soft-bodied insects and insect eggs throughout the summer. They are helpful in greenhouses where they attack thrips, aphids, mites, and scales. Their long proboscis digs deep into flower buds, searching out tasty thrips to eat.

Boxelder or maple bug

Leptocoris trivittatus

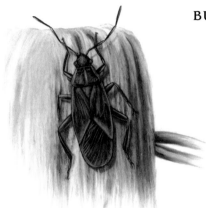

BUG AT A GLANCE

TYPE OF BUG: scentless plant bug

SIZE: about 12 mm (½ in.) long

WHAT IT LOOKS LIKE: nymph is bright red; adult is a dull black bug with red markings outlining wings and thorax

WHERE YOU FIND IT: boxelders (Manitoba maple), walls, and fences

WHEN YOU FIND IT: usually the nymph appears in June; adult appears from July through September

WHAT IT EATS: nymph and adult pierce leaf tissue and suck moisture from leaves

FRIEND OR FOE: relatively benign; large numbers alarm some people

WHAT TO DO: ignore it; if you must, hose from surfaces with a hard spray of water

BUG BIO

These prairie natives undergo gradual metamorphosis. In spring, adults lay bright red eggs on the leaves of boxelder, other maples, and ash trees. The emerging red nymphs suck the sap from leaves of these trees. The nymphs mature through five molts, resembling the adult more with each succeeding molt. Flying adults emerge by late summer or fall, often in very large numbers. The adults pierce plant tissue and suck juice from leaves and seeds, but do relatively little harm. They tend to cluster on warm fences and walls, which worries some people. The adult bugs usually overwinter under debris and the loose bark of trees although some may prefer to overwinter in your home.

Tarnished plant bug

Lygus lineolaris

BUG AT A GLANCE (no illustration)
  TYPE OF BUG: lygus plant bug
  SIZE: about 5 mm (⅕ in.) long
  WHAT IT LOOKS LIKE: oval, bronzy-colored bug with a distinctive white triangle or V-shape behind the head
  WHERE YOU FIND IT: a number of crop and ornamental plants; roses are a very common victim
  WHEN YOU FIND IT: adult appears in early June, second generation appears from June to mid-July
  WHAT IT EATS: nymph and adult suck plant juices
  FRIEND OR FOE: foe
  WHAT TO DO: clear weeds to eliminate breeding sites; remove parts of plants most affected

BUG BIO
Tarnished plant bugs overwinter as adults beneath suitable cover. In the spring they become active and disperse to feed on early-emerging plants. After mating, females lay individual eggs in plant tissue. There may be two generations in the southern prairies, and only one in the north.

These bugs pierce plant tissue and suck juices from a plant, which can cause wilting. Many plants react to the toxin in the bug's saliva by developing deformities or bud drop.

In addition to the tarnished plant bug, there are several other species of lygus bugs on the prairies and they have similarly nasty habits. A related bug, the bright red superb plant bug (*Adelphocoris superbus*), can be a pest of alfalfa crops, but is not a threat to your garden treasures.

Stink bug

Family Pentatomidae

BUG AT A GLANCE
  TYPE OF BUG: stink bug
  SIZE: about 10 mm (⅜ in.) long

Stink bug (Family Pentatomidae)

WHAT IT LOOKS LIKE: shield-shaped, yellowish brown or green bug
WHERE YOU FIND IT: mostly on trees and shrubs, commonly willow and birch
WHEN YOU FIND IT: nymph appears in late June and early July
WHAT IT EATS: nymph pierces leaf and sucks leaf sap
FRIEND OR FOE: minor foe
WHAT TO DO: hose tree down; use contact insecticide if necessary

BUG BIO
Females lay their eggs in the spring; they are very protective of their eggs and young nymphs. The round or flat nymhs may be a different colour from the adults. Stink bugs overwinter as adults in the debris under trees.

Some stink bugs are predators; others gain nourishment from plant juices. The resultant mottled foliage is unsightly and leaves might drop a little early, but these bugs cause no appreciable damage to trees.

Stink bugs can, indeed, stink. They produce organic volatile liquids as a defensive measure against natural predators. Each species has its own characteristic stink.

The prairies are home to several species of stink bugs, each with its own preferred plant or animal food.

Green peach aphid

Myzus persicae

BUG AT A GLANCE
   TYPE OF BUG: aphid
   SIZE: pinhead
   WHAT IT LOOKS LIKE: translucent, usually green, pear-shaped insect
   WHERE YOU FIND IT: in clusters on leaves or buds of many garden plants
   WHEN YOU FIND IT: spring to fall; 20 to 30 generations
   WHAT IT EATS: plant sap
   FRIEND OR FOE: foe

WHAT TO DO: hose down frequently with a hard spray of water; remove tender new leaves where aphids are most numerous

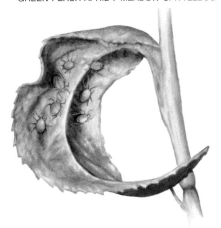

Green peach aphid (*Myzus persicae*)

BUG BIO

Aphids overwinter as eggs and the nymphs that emerge in spring are all wingless females. These aphids produce more female aphids directly, which produce more female aphids ... all summer long. In the fall, a generation of winged males and females is produced. They mate, lay eggs, and die. The eggs overwinter on plant stems and the cycle continues the following spring.

Aphids suck the vital juices from your plants, causing leaves to curl, wilt, and eventually die. They secrete a sticky substance known as honeydew, of which some species of ants are enormously fond. Ants will protect and herd "their" aphids to ensure a constant supply of honeydew. The sooty mold that commonly develops on honeydew is unsightly. Aphids can also spread viruses that are difficult to control. Give lady beetles and other predators a chance to control aphids by not spraying insecticides. The damage aphids do in your garden is usually more unsightly than serious.

Meadow spittlebug

Philaenus spumarius

BUG AT A GLANCE (no illustration)

TYPE OF BUG: spittlebug

SIZE: 10 mm (⅜ in.) long

WHAT IT LOOKS LIKE: adult is grayish green, said to resemble a tiny frog; nymph conceals itself in a blob of spittle

WHERE YOU FIND IT: at leaf axils, sheaths of grass stems in meadows, gardens, and cropland

WHEN YOU FIND IT: June and July

WHAT IT EATS: nymph eats leaves, shoots, and stems of many plants

FRIEND OR FOE: minor foe

WHAT TO DO: hose plant down if you really must

BUG BIO

Eggs hatch in the spring, and newly emerged nymphs protect themselves with a foamy covering, which they produce by mixing plant juices with juices from their glands. As the liquid exits a spittlebug's anus, it mixes with air to form bubbles, which may make them an instant hit with your kids.

Winged adults hop like tiny frogs. They are seen on shrubs and are quite unsightly (especially if you have a good imagination), but they do little damage. Spittlebugs overwinter as eggs on branches or leaf stems.

The foamy covering that makes the nymphs so distinctive serves as protection against predators. Some birds have learned to pick the nymph from the spittle blob, and some parasitic insects are, likewise, undeterred.

Virginia creeper leafhopper

Erythroneura ziczac

BUG AT A GLANCE

TYPE OF BUG: leafhopper
SIZE: 6 mm (¼ in.) long
WHAT IT LOOKS LIKE: elongated, green aphidlike creature with a pointy rear end and a pronounced hump near the head
WHERE YOU FIND IT: on Virginia creeper, Engelmann ivy, and hops
WHEN YOU FIND IT: July
WHAT IT EATS: nymph sucks sap from leaves
FRIEND OR FOE: foe; ruins appearance of plant
WHAT TO DO: learn to live with it or plant something else; use a well-aimed spray from the hose frequently

BUG BIO

Aphids are bad enough, but what about super-aphids that jump? The translucent, pale green leafhoppers look somewhat like elongated aphids, but their pointy rear ends give them away. That, and the fact that they jump when disturbed. The powerful back legs have rows of spines.

Virginia creeper leafhoppers lay their eggs on leaves in early spring and cover them with a light blue material that protects them from predation. Pale, greenish yellow nymphs emerge in spring and begin feeding on the leaf undersides of Virginia creeper, Engelmann ivy, or hops. White spots on the top surface of the leaves reveal their existence. Mature adults are present by midsummer; they overwinter in leaf litter.

Although these horrid little creatures do little permanent harm to the plants, they do deny you the beautiful red fall coloration of the Virginia creeper that you have waited for all year. Instead, the leaves turn brown and crunchy as the result of leafhopper damage.

If an infested vine is growing against a solid fence or wall, it is difficult to use an insecticide to get rid of them, as they are found only on leaf undersides. You might have better luck by sticking a hose through the branches at the bottom of the vine, aiming it upward between the wall and the vine, and giving them a hard spray of water. This may dislodge most leafhoppers; spraying frequently can keep them under control.

Western flower thrips

Frankliniella occidentalis

BUG AT A GLANCE (no illustration)

TYPE OF BUG: thrips

SIZE: 1 to 2 mm ($\frac{1}{25}$ to $\frac{1}{10}$ in.) long

WHAT IT LOOKS LIKE: slender, tiny insect, with four narrow, fuzzy wings

WHERE YOU FIND IT: flowers and their buds; often in greenhouses

WHEN YOU FIND IT: first generation appears in June; several generations

WHAT IT EATS: mostly sap of flower petals

FRIEND OR FOE: a nasty foe

WHAT TO DO: difficult to control but it has many natural enemies; soak gladioli corms in a mild disinfectant solution before planting

BUG BIO

Flower thrips are common on garden flowers, but there is nothing nice to say about them. Thrips lay their eggs amongst foliage. They multiply very quickly, deforming flower petals and buds and making it impractical to bring flowers indoors. The nymphs pierce plant tissue and suck the vital plant juices. After the nymphs have eaten their fill, they drop to the ground to pupate.

The usual indication of thrips' damage is light-colored spots on the leaves where they have been feeding. Roses are a favorite place to live; white roses the best place of all. Thrips have many predators, including lacewings, minute pirate bugs, and hover flies, so using an insecticide might kill more predators than thrips.

There are many species of thrips, each with a different preferred host and a unique life cycle. The gladiolus thrips (*Taeniothrips simplex*) is a severe scourge of gladioli. This thrips, which is dark colored with a distinctive white band at the base of the fore wings, overwinters on gladiolus corms. Infested glads show poor growth and have fewer flowers, buds that may not open, and leaves and flowers streaked with silver. This thrips can be preempted by soaking the corms in a mild disinfectant solution like Lysol™ for a few hours or overnight just before planting. Use one part disinfectant to ten parts water.

Recently, scientists discovered that some species of thrips may be eusocial, meaning that they have complex societies with more than one caste, the same as ants or bees.

One Thrips, Two Thrips

You would never see just one of these little creatures, but if you did, it would still be a thrips, not a thrip.

Green lacewing

Order Neuroptera
Family Crysopidae

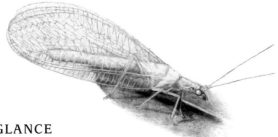

BUG AT A GLANCE

TYPE OF BUG: lacewing

SIZE: 10 to 25 mm (⅜ to 1 in.) long

WHAT IT LOOKS LIKE: green insect with gold eyes and large, iridescent, delicately veined wings

WHERE YOU FIND IT: plants where its prey lives

WHEN YOU FIND IT: early spring to late summer

WHAT IT EATS: adult and nymph eat insects, especially aphids
FRIEND OR FOE: a dear and wonderful friend
WHAT TO DO: appreciate its beauty and usefulness

BUG BIO

These beautiful pale green insects are often called aphid lions because they are voracious consumers of aphids. Nymphs and adults also eat spider mites, leafhoppers, small caterpillars, thrips, and some insect eggs. The adult female lays eggs that are attached to vegetation by distinctive stalks. The sturdy larvae are alligatorlike creatures with sharp pincers. These resourceful nymphs may attach the dead husk of their vanquished prey to their back as concealment. Amongst the first predators to appear in spring, lacewings are very important in suppressing the early generations of aphids.

The adults are largely nocturnal and may come indoors, attracted by light. Some species have bat-detecting, ultrasonic sound receptors in their wing veins.

Another family of lacewings, the brown lacewings (Family Hemerobiidae), have a similar lifestyle. They are smaller than green lacewings, being 4 to 12 mm (⅛ to ½ in.) long.

Lady beetle, ladybug, or ladybird beetle

Family Coccinellidae

BUG AT A GLANCE

TYPE OF BUG: beetle
SIZE: usually 4 to 6 mm (⅛ to ¼ in.) long
WHAT IT LOOKS LIKE: adult is a bright red or orange, almost round beetle, with varying numbers of black spots; larva is a longish, alligatorlike creature with bumps
WHERE YOU FIND IT: anywhere aphids occur, often birch, boxelder (Manitoba maple), apple, and elm trees
WHEN YOU FIND IT: spring to fall
WHAT IT EATS: beetle and larva eat mostly aphids
FRIEND OR FOE: a very good friend
WHAT TO DO: treasure it and don't endanger it with pesticides

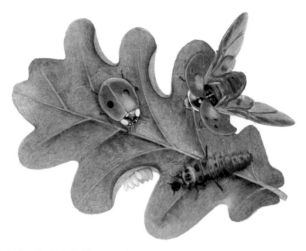

Two-spotted lady beetle (*Adalia bipunctata*), seven-spotted lady beetle (*Coccinella septempunctata*)

BUG BIO

Lady beetles are recognized by many people as "good for the garden," but few know about the many species that live on the prairies, and even fewer know what the larvae look like. These wonderful beetles can wear a variety of spots and several wing colors. There are red lady beetles with no spots, and some with two, seven, twelve, or even more spots. There are also pale yellow ones, and black ones with two red spots, which are known as "twice-stabbed lady beetles."

When you see lady beetles, look carefully to find their hard-working kids. The larvae in no way resemble their parents and are often assumed to be a problem. In fact, they eat more aphids than mum and dad. They are long and dark, with colored bumps on their backs, and resemble tiny alligators.

Lady beetles can squirt a bad-tasting, smelly blood from thin spots along their jointed legs when frightened. It's a good defense, and birds and spiders don't bother them twice. Ants like the sticky secretions produced by aphids, and will protect them, often attacking lady beetles.

There are twenty or more species of lady beetle that are easily recognized and about seventy-five species in all on the prairies. Each has a distinctive number of spots or markings on the wings. Many are native; some are not. There is mounting evidence that the non-native, seven-spot lady beetle might be out-competing or hybridizing with the native transverse lady beetle (*Coccinella transversoguttata*). You are most likely to encounter the two-spotted lady beetle, a native, and the seven-spotted lady beetle, an introduced species.

The two-spotted lady beetle (*Adalia bipunctata*) is smaller than the seven-spotted one, and almost round in shape. These beetles fly well and spend the summers in trees and large shrubs, eating aphids. The eggs are yellow, and the larvae are black with yellow and white spots. Two-spotted lady beetles often overwinter indoors and appear on warm windows in the spring, ready to get outside as soon as it is warm enough for them. In the meantime, they might just eat a few aphids on your houseplants.

The seven-spotted lady beetle (*Coccinella septempunctata*) is generally larger than the two-spotted one and oval in shape. Their eggs are orange and oval-shaped, and laid in clusters on the underside of leaves. The alligatorlike larvae are dark with orange spots. Seven-spotted lady beetles can be bought commercially and turned loose in your garden. Unfortunately, they are poor fliers, so spend much of their time on plants close to the ground. Fortunately, if there are aphids in your garden (and you haven't sprayed insecticides there recently), lady beetles will come of their own accord. You might also remember the childhood poem "Ladybird, ladybird, fly away home." There is no guarantee that the ones you paid for and lovingly released in your garden won't think that the aphids are greener on the other side of the fence. So welcome those that visit your garden.

Adults overwinter in winter mulch and debris close to the ground. Don't be too eager to remove this ground cover in the spring, as the lady beetles need protection from sudden spring frosts.

Seeing Spots

- Did you know that lady beetles are very pale and have no spots for the first twenty-four hours of their lives?
- Have you heard that you can tell how old a lady beetle is by the number of spots on its back? Sorry, it isn't true. The number of spots is dictated by the species.
- Are you surprised to learn that there are four hundred species of lady beetles in North America?

Nuttall's blister beetle

Lytta nuttalli

BUG AT A GLANCE

TYPE OF BUG: blister beetle
SIZE: 15 to 20 mm (⅝ to ¾ in.) long
WHAT IT LOOKS LIKE: long, narrow, greenish purple, metallic-colored beetle

WHERE YOU FIND IT: on the ground, on food plants
WHEN YOU FIND IT: larva feeds in late July and August
WHAT IT EATS: foliage of legumes; grasshopper eggs; leafcutter bee larvae
FRIEND OR FOE: friend and foe (does eating grasshopper eggs make up for eating beneficial leafcutter bee larvae?)
WHAT TO DO: put the bug spray away

Nuttall's blister beetle
(*Lytta nuttalli*)

BUG BIO

Adult blister beetles emerge from the soil in early summer and move to food plants. Females lay eggs in clusters and the larvae that hatch eat grasshopper eggs (good!) and bumblebee and leafcutter bee larvae (bad!). Mature larvae overwinter as hard-shelled larvae. Their life cycle is unusual in that the overwintering hard-cased larva reverts to a soft larva before undergoing true pupation.

Nuttall's blister beetles are attractive, metallic-colored, narrow beetles that are most common on legume crops, such as beans, alfalfa and canola, and on weeds, such as vetch and locoweed. A similar species, the caragana blister beetle (*Lytta viridana*) feeds on caragana. Swarms of blister beetles can be detrimental to food crops and also lessen the pollination of alfalfa crops if leafcutter bee larvae are destroyed. Caragana hedges and windbreaks can be defoliated but only young plants are seriously affected.

Spanishfly

Blister beetles produce a potent chemical called cantharadin, which can cause blistering on skin. A certain European blister beetle has been ground up over the centuries and sold as "spanishfly" to gullible people as a cure for nearly every imaginable illness or condition and, most famously, as an aphrodisiac. Actually, the effect on the private parts of duped males is not at all pleasant and unlikely to result in amorous adventures.

Delphinium or larkspur leaftier

Polychrysia esmeralda

BUG AT A GLANCE (no illustration)

TYPE OF BUG: noctuid moth caterpillar

SIZE: about 6 mm (¼ in.)

WHAT IT LOOKS LIKE: small, green caterpillar

WHERE YOU FIND IT: the growing tips of delphinium, monkshood, or larkspur

WHEN YOU FIND IT: caterpillar leaf damage appears in June when plants are about 30 cm (12 in.) high

WHAT IT EATS: caterpillar eats delphinium, monkshood, or larkspur

FRIEND OR FOE: foe of delphinium and monkshood gardeners

WHAT TO DO: handpick; pinch affected tips; use insecticidal dusts; hope that birds find it

BUG BIO

It is not the caterpillar or the adult moth that will get your attention, but rather the disfigured growing tips of your delphiniums and their relatives. The moth responsible for this alarming situation lays her eggs near the base of a delphinium or related plant. In the spring, the young caterpillars travel up the inside of the plant stem and lodge themselves in the developing bud region. As a result, new growth appears tight and curled, black excrement eventually appears on the growing tips, and the plant fails to develop properly.

Distasteful as it may be, the best control is handpicking. Gently unroll the curled leaves and pick out the small, green caterpillars. Alternatively, pinch off the tip of the plant. It will recover. Some sources suggest cutting the plants back hard, which does work, but it delays flowering in the short prairie growing season. Insecticidal dusts can also be used. Some birds also learn to recognize a good thing and will visit your plants looking for tasty morsels.

(Delphinium leaftier identification from Ernest Mengerson, Olds College, personal communication.)

Yellow woollybear caterpillar

Lophocampa maculata

BUG AT A GLANCE

TYPE OF BUG: tiger moth caterpillar
SIZE: 32 mm (about 1¼ in.) long
WHAT IT LOOKS LIKE: large, furry caterpillar with three sections of color (black, orange, black) and coarser tufts of white bristles
WHERE YOU FIND IT: anywhere, often vegetable gardens
WHEN YOU FIND IT: summer
WHAT IT EATS: caterpillar eats flowers, vegetables, and weeds
FRIEND OR FOE: benign
WHAT TO DO: leave it alone; parasitic wasps and birds eat caterpillars

BUG BIO

Woollybears are well-known, endearing fuzzy creatures. Gardeners are less familiar with the adult, which is a tiger moth. The moth is tan, with brown patches and spots, and has a 25 to 50 mm (1 to 2 in.) wingspan. Its antennae are long and comblike.

Woollybear caterpillars overwinter as pupae in protected areas. The moths emerge in spring and mate. Eggs hatch in a week and caterpillars feed on leaf undersides. After a month, the caterpillars are mature and find a sheltered place to pupate.

"Woollybear" is a very imprecise name sometimes applied to caterpillars of various tiger moths. The "true" woollybear (if you can apply this judgment to a common name) is the Isabella tiger moth caterpillar (*Pyrrharctica isabella*). This caterpillar has a red band between black ends and no white tufts. It can be found in the prairie region.

Caterpillar with a Crystal Ball

A long-cherished notion is that the severity of the impending winter can be foretold by the relative width of the red band of the woolly bear caterpillar: the wider the red band, the milder the coming winter. It has become an annual ritual in some parks, schools, and institutions to round up woolly bears each fall and count their segments. Although this exercise is mainly done for fun, it is an intriguing way to pique kids' interest in insects.

Leafcutter bee

Family Megachilidae

BUG AT A GLANCE (illustration of symptoms, p. 36)

TYPE OF BUG: solitary bee

SIZE: 6 to 20 mm (¼ to ¾ in.) long

WHAT IT LOOKS LIKE: a stout, small to medium-sized bee of various colors

WHERE YOU FIND IT: widely distributed wherever nectar-producing flowers are found

WHEN YOU FIND IT: adult not usually noticed; holes in leaves appear in spring and summer

WHAT IT EATS: larva feeds on nectar and pollen supplied by the adult female

FRIEND OR FOE: friend

WHAT TO DO: get your kids and try to observe this bee in action

BUG BIO

It's hard to believe that a bee can chew perfectly round and oblong holes in the leaves of roses. The leafcutter bee that chews holes in your roses looks like a small, black wasp. The female uses the leaf pieces to line egg cells. To lay her eggs, she chooses a narrow, tubular cavity, such as a hollow plant cane or a hole bored in wood. Inside the cavity, she prepares a special cell for each egg. She lines each cell with an elongated leaf piece and caps the ends with the round pieces. Then, inside each cell, she places an egg with a supply of pollen and some honey. In the end, the rose doesn't miss a few bits of leaf and, although the leaves look like big, fat caterpillars have attacked them, no harm is done.

Like honeybees, these bees can sting, but they are not very aggressive and their sting is said to be not as painful.

Leafcutter bees are valuable pollinators. The alfalfa leafcutter bee (*Megachile rotundata*) was accidentally introduced into North America from Eurasia, most likely during World War II, with crated war materials. It has since proved a valuable asset to western farmers as an alfalfa crop pollinator.

Are Those Outhouses?

As you drive through the prairies, you may see fields with rows of open sheds. These sheds are man-made accommodations for the alfalfa leafcutter bee, which is employed by farmers for pollinating alfalfa crops.

Goldenrod crab spider

Family Thomisidae
Misumena vatia

BUG AT A GLANCE (illustration p. 172)
TYPE OF BUG: crab spider
SIZE: female is up to 10 mm (⅜ in.) long; males are much smaller
WHAT IT LOOKS LIKE: white or yellow spider with very long front legs and indentations on the carapace
WHERE YOU FIND IT: inside a yellow or white flower
WHEN YOU FIND IT: adult usually appears in summer
WHAT IT EATS: flying insects
FRIEND OR FOE: friend and foe; a predator that eats both "bad" and "good" bugs
WHAT TO DO: allow it to take its natural place in the web of life

BUG BIO
Crab spiders really are somewhat crab shaped and can walk sideways and backwards. Many of them specialize in lurking inside flowers and grabbing unsuspecting bees, flies, or butterflies that come for nectar. The goldenrod crab spider is famous for its ability to change from white to yellow and back again to suit the color of its background. It takes a few days for the spider to accomplish this feat.

Crab spiders do not spin a web, but like all spiders, they are capable of spinning silk. The female crab spider uses silk for making an egg sac. She usually dies before the spiderlings emerge. The males of some species wisely wrap the aggressive female loosely in silk during mating.

Jumping Spider

Family Salticidae

BUG AT A GLANCE (illustration p. 172)
TYPE OF BUG: jumping spider
SIZE: 3 to 15 mm (⅛ to ⅝ in.), usually on the small side
WHAT IT LOOKS LIKE: small, fuzzy spider with large, forward-facing

eyes; appears to sit up on tall front legs; male often has brightly marked fore legs

WHERE YOU FIND IT: on plants and on windowsills

WHEN YOU FIND IT: spring to fall

WHAT IT EATS: any small insect it can pounce on

FRIEND OR FOE: benign; an endearing creature

WHAT TO DO: have no fear

BUG BIO

If toy companies made stuffed spiders, they would look like jumping spiders. Even the most spider-loathing gardener has to admit that little jumping spiders are downright cute, with their fuzzy bodies and large, forward-facing eyes. They actually have eight eyes, but the largest pair sits up front and looks like our eyes. These large eyes are not just for show; jumping spiders have the best eyesight amongst spiders. It is thought that they can see detailed images up to 30 cm (12 in.) away. They can also swivel their head to get a good look around. Some researchers have reported that a jumping spider perched on a field notebook will follow the movement of pen on paper with a keen interest.

Jumping spiders can spy potential prey from some distance away, slowly creeping up to it until they make their final pounce. Although they don't produce a web, they do lay out a dragline behind them, which they can use to reel themselves back up if necessary.

Like many female spiders, the female jumping spiders are usually in hunting mode and need to be properly courted to get in the mood for love. When a male spider intent on mating approaches, he needs to communicate this to the female to ensure that she doesn't mistake him for a meal. The males of many species have exuberantly colored and tufted front legs that they use like semaphore flags to signal their amorous intent. Each species has its own particular set of signals. If the female is suitably impressed, the male can then come forward to mate.

Harvestman or daddy longlegs

Order Opiliones

BUG AT A GLANCE

TYPE OF BUG: an arachnid, but not a spider

SIZE: body is 4 to 6 mm (⅛ to ¼ in.) long

WHAT IT LOOKS LIKE: a spiderlike bug with eight very long legs;

oval-shaped body is brown with markings

WHERE YOU FIND IT: everywhere in the garden

WHEN YOU FIND IT: towards late summer when it is large

WHAT IT EATS: small insects, dead or decaying organic matter

FRIEND OR FOE: friend

WHAT TO DO: be gentle, although it may not be as fragile as it looks

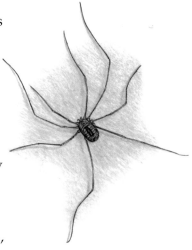

BUG BIO

Although similar to spiders in many ways, harvestmen show some distinct differences. The cephalothorax is closely fused to the abdomen, giving them the appearance of

Harvestman (Order Opiliones)

having only one body part, rather than two like spiders. They have a pair of eyes on short stalks. They have no spinnerets and cannot produce silk. They possess a pair of chelicerae but they do not usually bite people, contrary to some lurid myths. Let harvestmen walk on you to impress your squeamish friends.

The female deposits eggs into moist soil with her ovipositor. In spring the young emerge and grow slowly. They are seldom noticed until late summer or fall when they are fully grown. The adults are sometimes seen in groups with legs interlaced. Harvestmen live for a year and die when the weather turns cold.

Goldenrod crab spider (*Misumena vatia*)
(p. 170)

Jumping spider (Family Salticidae)
(p. 170)

13

THE VEGGIE VISITORS

There is a small group of bugs that enjoys your vegetables as much as you do. A few of those most likely to be encountered by the prairie vegetable gardener are presented in this section.

Tuber flea beetle

Epitrix tuberis

BUG AT A GLANCE

TYPE OF BUG: leaf beetle
SIZE: 2 mm (⅒ in.) long
WHAT IT LOOKS LIKE: tiny, dull black beetle
WHERE YOU FIND IT: in soil where potatoes are grown
WHEN YOU FIND IT: adult seen in mid-June
WHAT IT EATS: larva eats potato tubers; beetle eats leaves
FRIEND OR FOE: foe of potato growers
WHAT TO DO: accept surface damage or don't grow potatoes; insecticides aren't safe enough to use on food

BUG BIO

Adult beetles overwinter in the soil and emerge in early summer. They feed on weeds until potato vegetation is available. They lay their eggs at the base of plants and hatch in a week. The larvae mature in the potato tuber for three to four weeks, and then pupate. Adults emerge in midsummer and feed on leaves until fall.

Tuber flea beetles chew tiny holes in the leaves of potato plants. They jump when disturbed, accounting for their common name. The larvae feed on potato tubers, but will also eat other vegetables if necessary. Their presence is not usually noticed until holes appear in the leaves, or until the pitted potatoes are dug up in the fall. Although damaged potatoes look unappealing, they are safe to eat. Just peel the potato a little more thickly than usual.

To prevent damage, pesticides must be used continuously in the soil, which is not an appealing solution. A better solution is to simply stop growing potatoes for a while. Instead, buy potatoes from a farmer's market or co-op and use the garden for growing something less troublesome for a few years.

Carrot rust fly

Psila rosae

BUG AT A GLANCE (no illustration)

TYPE OF BUG: psilid or rust fly

SIZE: 6 mm (¼ in.) long

WHAT IT LOOKS LIKE: small, straw-colored maggot; adult is a slender, shiny black fly with clear wings

WHERE YOU FIND IT: where carrots are grown

WHEN YOU FIND IT: damage is seen when carrots are harvested; the insects are not noticed aboveground

WHAT IT EATS: maggot eats carrots

FRIEND OR FOE: foe

WHAT TO DO: use row covers to prevent the fly from entering soil near carrots

BUG BIO

Carrot rust flies overwinter as pupae in the soil. Adults emerge in June, move to plants in sheltered places, and begin to feed and mate. The female deposits her eggs near carrot plants in the evening. Carrot rust fly maggots are attracted to the carbon dioxide emitted by carrot plants. They feed on the small roots of the carrot, which can kill young carrots and make older ones stunted or forked. Older maggots enter the roots and tunnel in the lower portion of the carrot. Fungi and bacteria can enter carrots through the open tunnels and make them inedible.

Chemical retaliation is unecessary, as there is a magical, perfectly safe way to prevent damage to the carrots. Row covers are made of very fine polyester fabric that allows water to penetrate and sunlight to shine through, but prevents the insects from reaching the plants. It is placed over the row where the carrots are planted and left somewhat loose so the carrots can push it up as they grow. Hold the row cover down on the edges with wood, bricks, etc. Leave it on until well into summer. If done properly, you won't have any carrot rust fly damage on your carrots.

Onion root maggot

Hylemya antiqua, syn. *Delia antiqua*

BUG AT A GLANCE (illustration of symptoms, p. 37)
   TYPE OF BUG: anthomyid fly
   SIZE: maggot is 10 mm (⅜ in.) long; adult is 7 mm (⅓ in.) long
   WHAT IT LOOKS LIKE: maggot has an off-white, tapered body; adult looks like a housefly with longer legs
   WHERE YOU FIND IT: in soil where onions are grown
   WHEN YOU FIND IT: maggots feed in June; several generations occur but are rarely seen
   WHAT IT EATS: maggot eats onion roots
   FRIEND OR FOE: foe to onion growers
   WHAT TO DO: move onions to different areas of your garden; encourage the presence of ground beetles and rove beetles by not using pesticides

BUG BIO

These flies overwinter as tiny pupae. Adults emerge in the spring when the weather is warm enough. The adults are attracted to the odor of onions, and feed on flowering weeds nearby. The females lay eggs under the soil surface, beneath onion plants. The maggots feed on onion roots before pupating in the soil. There can be up to three generations per year. Ornamental alliums can also fall victim to the onion root maggot, although, since they are not regularly dug up, you may not recognize onion root maggot damage on them.

Ground beetles and rove beetles eat the eggs of onion maggots. Practice crop rotation by moving onions to different areas of your garden each year to break the cycle.

Colorado potato beetle

Leptinotarsa decemlineata

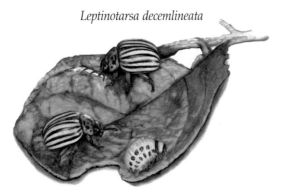

BUG AT A GLANCE

TYPE OF BUG: leaf beetle

SIZE: adult and grub are 6 to 12 mm (¼ to ½ in.) long

WHAT IT LOOKS LIKE: long, oval, yellow beetle with black stripes; yellowish clumps of eggs on underside of leaves; reddish larva with black spots; pupa resembles a motionless orange blob

WHERE YOU FIND IT: on potato plants; all stages likely to be seen, often together

WHEN YOU FIND IT: adult appears in late May or June; a second generation often occurs

WHAT IT EATS: foliage of potato plants, occasionally the foliage of tomato plants

FRIEND OR FOE: foe; can do a great deal of damage to potatoes

WHAT TO DO: handpick; use insecticidal dusts

BUG BIO

Adult beetles emerge in early summer and fly to food sources; they usually eat potatoes, but can also attack other plants in the nightshade family, such as tomatoes. Females lay hundreds of eggs on leaf undersides and then die. Adult beetles overwinter well beneath the soil surface. They are more likely to survive with heavy snow cover for insulation.

Both the larvae and adults eat foliage. If their numbers are large in the early stages of plant growth, potatoes may not develop good tubers and tomatoes may not fruit. If plants have a chance to flower, less damage occurs. The beetles can also carry difficult-to-control diseases to plants. Handpicking is effective in gardens, as is the use of insecticidal dusts. Only use dusts on the foliage when beetles are present.

O Pioneer Beetle

Before settlers invaded the American southwest, the Colorado potato beetle was an innocuous little beetle feeding on buffalo bur, a species of solanum related to the potato. As settlers began growing potatoes, the little beetle found huge quantities of a new host that was very much to its liking. With this bonanza, the beetle spread rapidly, perhaps 130 km (80 mi.) a year. By the 1870s, it had invaded eastern North America, and since World War I, it has become abundant in Russia and Asia as well.

Imported cabbageworm

Pieris rapae

BUG AT A GLANCE (illustration p. 68)

TYPE OF BUG: cabbage white butterfly caterpillar

SIZE: caterpillar is 30 mm (1¼ in.) long

WHAT IT LOOKS LIKE: caterpillar has a velvety skin and light yellow, broken lines down the back

WHERE YOU FIND IT: cabbage and other cruciferous vegetables

WHEN YOU FIND IT: butterfly first seen in mid-May; caterpillar first appears in mid-June; there may be several generations

WHAT IT EATS: caterpillar eats cabbage leaves

FRIEND OR FOE: foe; the "kids" are a nuisance but the adult is quite pretty

WHAT TO DO: apply bacterial insecticide such as BTk; natural predators such as braconid wasps can help to control them

BUG BIO

Eggs are laid in late May on cabbage plant leaves. Caterpillars begin feeding on the leaves and mature in about three weeks. Jagged-edged holes in leaves indicate the presence of caterpillars. Caterpillars pupate by sticking to fences, walls, or any vertical surface. Adult butterflies are easily seen flying over cabbage plants, other common garden vegetables, and some flowers such as nasturtium and carnation. There can be several generations a year if the weather is warm. They overwinter as a chrysalis in debris on the ground.

Diamondback moth caterpillar

Plutella xylostella

BUG AT A GLANCE (no illustration)

TYPE OF BUG: diamondback moth caterpillar
SIZE: larva is about 12 mm (½ in.) long at maturity
WHAT IT LOOKS LIKE: small, pale green caterpillar
WHERE YOU FIND IT: leaves of vegetables where canola is grown
WHEN YOU FIND IT: damage most noticeable in late July; three or more generations occur
WHAT IT EATS: caterpillar eats leaves and flowers of crucifers
FRIEND OR FOE: an introduced foe
WHAT TO DO: hose off small caterpillars and hope for rain

BUG BIO

This diamondback moth is small and light brown, with white, diamond-shaped markings on the wings. They lay their eggs in spring on either side of canola leaves, which hatch soon after. The tiny caterpillars move into the leaf and feed on its tissue for a week or so, then move to the outer surface and continue feeding on the leaf undersides for several weeks. Lacy, white pupae are very numerous. Adults emerge in one to two weeks and begin laying eggs immediately.

Like many problem insects, this is an introduced species. There can be several generations in a summer, but they do not survive the winter in the northern prairies. The moths are carried north by wind from the south. The first generation usually arrives before the first canola crop is edible, so the eggs are laid on leaves of weeds or crucifers. The second generation feeds on canola crops for most of the summer. Later generations feed on available vegetables or canola in the area. Root vegetables will show little damage, but leafy vegetables can be unsightly to inedible.

In cool, wet weather many caterpillars fall from plants and drown. Cool temperatures also reduce the number of eggs that are laid, another factor affecting how numerous the caterpillars are in a particular season.

Diamondback moth caterpillar and imported cabbageworm damage is similar. If the holes are small and covered with a transparent "window," then the culprit is likely the diamondback moth caterpillar; if the holes are larger and there is no "window," then it's more likely the imported cabbageworm may be the guilty party.

14

THE WEB WEAVERS

S piders need a decent PR agent. With the exception of Charlotte, spiders are cast consistently as evildoers. But the truth is that they are neither stalkers nor poisoners of decent folk, and they live fascinating lives.

Orb-web weavers

Family Araneidae

BUG AT A GLANCE

TYPE OF BUG: spider

SIZE: female is up to 15 mm (⅝ in.) in diameter, not including legs; male is much smaller

WHAT THEY LOOK LIKE: spiders with a globular, brown to orange colored abdomen; species have various patterns on the abdomen

WHERE YOU FIND THEM: various places, depending on species

WHEN YOU FIND THEM: most noticeable in summer

WHAT THEY EAT: insects caught in their webs

FRIEND OR FOE: benign; both "good" and "bad" insects are caught in its web

WHAT TO DO: appreciate the beauty of the web and try to identify the spider that made it

BUG BIO

Orb-web weavers spin the well-organized web that inspires the nature photographer. When observed early in the morning, each web is a dew-spangled work of art. Yet, despite its intricacy, many orb-weavers weave a new web each night, often eating the old tattered one. The web's radial lines are made of dry silk, and the spiral lines are sticky. The spider avoids sticking to its own web by scampering along the dry radial threads. The spider also has an oiliness that helps to keep it free of its own sticky silk.

Some species sit boldly in the hub of their web, while others are more

circumspect, hiding nearby in a concealed crevice or leafy nest. When an
insect becomes entangled in the web,
the spider scampers over to its prey. If
the prey is small, it is quickly wrapped
in silk and transported to a suitable
spot to be eaten right away or saved
for later. A larger prey is treated more
carefully and may be subdued by a
poisonous bite before being wrapped
in silk. Some large insects like vespid
wasps may be carefully cut free of the
web, as they are too dangerous for the
spider to tackle. This should ease some
gardeners' fears. If a spider isn't willing to deal with a wasp, it definit-
ley won't be interested in dealing with a gardener either.

Most araneids live for only a year. The small male sometimes makes
his web close to a female's web. Mating can be a perilous adventure for
the male. Since araneids relate to their surroundings mostly by touch, the
male approaches the female's web carefully. He tugs the lines of her web
in ways that communicate his amorous intent, as he does not want to be
mistaken for a meal. It is true that male spiders are sometimes eaten after
mating, but this is not necessarily a bad thing. The males of many species
die soon after mating anyway, and providing the mother with a decent
meal of their own spent bodies at a time when she needs it most gives
her a better chance of raising successful offspring.

After mating successfully, the female hangs her egg sac near the web
in some concealed place. The spiderlings disperse when they emerge
from the egg sac. They are already encoded with complete web-building
instructions and build tiny webs similar to their parents' webs.

There are dozens of species of orb-weavers on the prairies. Next time
a large spider sits down beside you, don't bolt from your tuffet. Instead,
take a look at her—she won't hurt you—and you may be surprised by
her beauty.

The female marbled orb-weaver (*Araneus marmoreus*) (illustrated) is
a large spider, with a body up to 19 mm (¾ in.) long. Her abdomen is
attractively marbled in purples and browns and there are several orange
spots near the midline. In spite of her striking appearance, she usually
hides in a leafy retreat or under bark near her web. This spider builds an
irregular, spiraling web in tall grasses or shrubs.

The light brown jewel spider (*Araneus gemmoides*) can be very
large, with an abdomen over 20 mm (¾ in.) long, which has two bumps

or horns on the front end of it. The abdomen also has a distinct light line running down the middle, which is crossed by a chevron-shaped marking. This spider likes to build its web on or near houses, especially where there is a light on at night. You may think such a large spider must be rare, foreign, fierce, or poisonous, but it is not guilty on all counts.

The banded argiope (*Argiope trifasciata*) is a large, distinctive, and especially beautiful spider. The female's body may be 25 mm (1 in.) long; the male is about a quarter her size. The abdomen is slightly elongated and pointed at the posterior end. The legs are strongly banded in silver or pale yellow, and there are similarly colored, longitudinal lines on the abdomen. The large web, constructed in low vegetation, has a zigzag pattern near its hub, which is called a stabilimentum. The spider hangs in the middle of the web.

Long-jawed orb-weavers

Family Tetragnathidae

BUG AT A GLANCE
TYPE OF BUG: spider
SIZE: body is 5 to 7 mm (⅕ to ⅓ in.) long
WHAT THEY LOOK LIKE: elongated spiders with long chelicerae
WHERE YOU FIND THEM: usually in grassy areas, often near water
WHEN YOU FIND THEM: most noticeable in summer
WHAT THEY EAT: small, flying insects including midges and mosquitoes
FRIEND OR FOE: friend
WHAT TO DO: do not disturb them if you can help it

BUG BIO
Long-jawed orb-weavers create webs similar to those of the araneid spiders. The webs tend to have an open hub. Each species has its own web placement strategy. The web may be vertical, inclined, or situated horizontally over water.

Long-jawed orb-weavers are named for their typically long fangs, properly called chelicerae. The males have especially long chelicerae, which they use to grip the female's chelicerae during mating. This prevents her from dining on him should she be in a surly mood.

These spiders often orient their front two pairs of legs forward, and the rear two pairs to the back, which enhances their overall elongated appearance. They are, thus, admirably camouflaged amongst grasses and reeds. Some of them hang downwards, looking like a piece of straw innocently tangled in the web.

The long-jawed orb-weaver (*Tetragnatha laboriosa*) (illustrated) is a relatively common member of the family. Both sexes are 5 to 6 mm (⅕ to ¼ in.) long. The cephalothorax is pale yellow, and the abdomen is silvery and striped with dark gray. The web is constructed between branches of shrubs and is usually inclined, sometimes almost horizontally. The spider stands to one side of the web, with its legs resting on the strands so it can detect the vibrations of any insects caught in the web.

Funnel-web weavers or grass spiders

Family Agelenidae
Agelenopsis spp.

BUG AT A GLANCE (illustration p. 184)

TYPE OF BUG: spider
SIZE: female is up to 20 mm (¾ in.) in diameter; male is slightly smaller
WHAT THEY LOOK LIKE: brown with a lighter, longitudinal stripe on the cephalothorax, and similar longitudinal stripes on the abdomen
WHERE YOU FIND THEM: in grassy areas
WHEN YOU FIND THEM: most noticeable in summer
WHAT THEY EAT: insects, especially grasshoppers
FRIEND OR FOE: friend
WHAT TO DO: investigate the ominous-looking web

BUG BIO

Grass spiders spin a thick, horizontal sheet web with a funnel at one edge. The web starts out small, but gets larger as the spider adds to it through its lifetime. There are overhead "trip" lines that serve to knock flying insects into the sheet. The sheet is not sticky and the spider must rush from the mouth of the funnel to capture its prey before it escapes. Grasshoppers are commonly caught this way. These spiders are shy and not often seen, as they remain deep inside the funnel of their web. Although webs are common in grassy areas, they may also be found well off the ground, and occasionally in buildings.

Tegenaria domestica, the house or cellar spider, lives up to its name and it is commonly found in houses and other buildings. Like some other species of *Tegenaria* it has been introduced from Europe and elsewhere. It finds our warm, dry buildings very much to its liking. Its thick, horizontal, triangular sheet web is often found in corners. In olden days, this spider's web was used to stanch the flow of blood from wounds.

House spiders are commonly found in tubs and sinks. They did not come up the drain, but rather, fell in, as they are not equipped with feet that can scale smooth, vertical surfaces. Rescue them and let them go outside. Even better, why not let them go in your basement where they will help rid dark corners of various crawlers? These spiders are not dangerous to people.

sheet-web weavers

Family Linyphiidae

BUG AT A GLANCE (no illustration)
TYPE OF BUG: spider
SIZE: 2 to 8 mm ($\frac{1}{10}$ to $\frac{1}{3}$ in.) in diameter, usually on the small side
WHAT THEY LOOK LIKE: very small, plain-colored, slightly elongated spider
WHERE YOU FIND THEM: dark places, often amongst leaf litter
WHEN YOU FIND THEM: most noticeable in summer
WHAT THEY EAT: small insects
FRIEND OR FOE: benign
WHAT TO DO: don't disturb them; unless you are a spider enthusiast, you will probably only notice their webs

BUG BIO
On the prairies there are far more species in this very large family than any other. These spiders are all very small and very unlikely to be noticed by anyone but those actively looking for them. They tend to prefer dark places and often live in leaf litter.

The webs are horizontal sheets or domes, often with a mesh of trip lines above. The spider normally hangs upside down under the web. Some species make another sheet below themselves, possibly for protection. When an insect hits the trip lines and falls onto the sheet, the spider runs over and pierces the prey with its fangs, right through the sheet. The stricken prey is then pulled through the sheet and bound with more silk. The diligent spider then repairs the hole in the web.

The hammock spider (*Pityohyphantes costatus*) makes a hammocklike web between branches or fence posts. Fallen leaves may be incorporated into the sheet.

Funnel-web weaver (*Agelenopsis* spp.) (p. 182)

Cobweb or comb-footed spiders

Family Theridiidae

BUG AT A GLANCE

TYPE OF BUG: spider

SIZE: 2 to 14 mm (⅒ to ⅝ in.) long

WHAT THEY LOOK LIKE: small to medium-sized, thickset spiders, with long slender legs; most have a light-colored abdomen; black widows are shiny black; female has a red, hour-glass marking on the dorsal side of the abdomen

WHERE YOU FIND THEM: many species found around buildings or debris; on plants

WHEN YOU FIND THEM: most noticeable in summer

WHAT THEY EAT: insects

FRIEND OR FOE: benign, except for the black widow

WHAT TO DO: check outhouses and debris piles for black widows

BUG BIO

Most species in this family spin the irregular, tangled webs we commonly call "cobwebs." The spiders tend to hang upside down below the webs. They are characterized by long legs and globular abdomens and are named for the comblike projections on their back legs. These combs are used for flinging silk over hapless victims.

Although there are many innocuous spiders in this family, it also includes the infamous western black widow spider (*Latrodectus hesperus*) (illustrated). This extremely attractive spider does indeed have highly toxic venom, but a bite from a black widow is generally not fatal. In spite of lurid tales, this spider is not aggressive, and bites occur when people unwittingly bother or otherwise surprise it. Only the female bites people. A good place for a web, from the spider's point of view, is under the seat of an outhouse. When outhouses were common on the prairies, men and boys were sometimes bitten on their private parts as they used the privy. Abandoned badger holes are another preferred place for a web.

Another spider in this family is the American house spider (*Achaearanea tepidariorum*). This spider is *not* dangerous to people. The females are 5 or 6 mm

(⅕ to ¼ in.) long and the males are slightly smaller. The abdomen of this spider varies from almost white to almost black, and the legs and cephalothorax are yellowish brown. The front legs are about three times as long as the body.

This spider is responsible for many of the irregular cobwebs found in buildings. A male and female may co-exist peaceably together on the same web. If the web is made in an unproductive place, the spider will abandon it and make a new one somewhere else. Unlike most spiders, it may live many years.

Spider Silk for Spiders

All spiders can make silk, which is produced from spinnerets on the bottom of the spider's abdomen. Spider silk is very versatile. Not all spiders make webs, but they all use silk in one or more innovative ways. For example:

- Spiderlings disperse by spinning a thin strand of silk that will eventually cause them to lift off in the slightest breeze, where air currents will carry them until they touch down somewhere else.
- Some spiders make themselves a dragline or a safety line, to which they stay attached while they go about their business.
- Meals may be bound with silk for later consumption.
- Eggs are usually wrapped in a silken cocoon.
- Nests may be lined with silk.

Spider Silk for People

Spider silk has long been recognized as having the combined characteristics of high strength, durability, and elasticity. (In many books it is said to be almost as strong as "fused quartz"—whatever that might be.) As well as being very, very strong, spider silk has been described as being five times finer and far more lustrous than silkworm silk. Yet, much to the dismay of entrepreneurs, and to the spider's benefit, a commercially viable way to use spider silk has not been developed, although some people have succeeded on a small scale. For example, in 1710, a Frenchman, M. Bon, unraveled silk from spiders and made some stockings and mittens with it. In the nineteenth century, some others found they could unravel silk directly from a hapless spider and spool it, getting as much as 135 m (150 yd.) from a single spider. The main problems (for humans, not for the spiders) is that none of our machines are fine enough to deal with spider silk, and spiders can't be kept together in huge numbers because they tend to eat each other.

GLOSSARY

Abdomen – the hind section of an insect or spider, containing the organs

Arachnid – a member of the order containing spiders, scorpions, mites, and harvestmen

Araneid – a spider, usually an orb-web weaver

Arthropoda – the group of animals containing insects, spiders, millipedes, centipedes, crustaceans, and others; an arthropod is the common term for any creature in the phylum Arthropoda

Biomass – the weight or mass of living organisms within a defined area

Cambium – the layer of cells between the bark and the wood of a tree that gives rise to new tree tissue

Carapace – a hard covering on the dorsal (top) side of an organism

Carbamates – a large group of synthetic organic insecticides containing hydrogen, carbon, and sulfur

Carboniferous – geologic age that occurred 360 to 285 million years ago

Carnivore – a meat-eating animal (including the meat of insects); carnivorous means meat-eating

Caterpillar – the juvenile stage of a moth or butterfly

Cephalothorax – the fused head and thorax of a spider

Chaetae – bristles on earthworms and related animals

Chelicerae – fangs of spiders and centipedes

Chitin – a complex molecule important in the exoskeleton of insects

Chlorinated hydrocarbons – a synthetic organic pesticide containing chlorine

Chrysalis – the pupa of a butterfly

Cocoon – a protective covering, often of silk, around the pupae of many insects, especially moths

Conifer – cone-bearing trees such as spruce, pine, and juniper; usually evergreen

Crawler – the juvenile stage of scale insects

Crop rotation – the practice of not planting the same vegetable crop in the same place two years in a row

Cruciferous – referring to plants in the cabbage or mustard family Cruciferae (e.g., cabbage, broccoli, and cauliflower), from "crux," or cross, referring to the four crosslike petals of the flowers

Deciduous – trees and shrubs that lose their leaves seasonally

Defoliate – remove leaves from

Diatomaceous earth – a product composed of the ground skeletons of diatoms, which are planktonic marine organisms; the sharp grains cut the bodies of soft-bodied pest organisms such as slugs

Dormant oil – a horticultural oil used on deciduous trees and shrubs when they are dormant (without leaves) to suffocate overwintering pests

Ecosystem – a contraction of "ecological system"; an integrated system of animals and plants, their habitat, and the processes that affect them

Elytra – the hard modified fore wings of beetles

Epigynum – the genital opening of a female spider

Exoskeleton – the external skeleton of arthropods

Exude – bleed

Floating row cover – a loose, breathable covering that is placed loosely over rows of vegetable crops to prevent attack by various pest insects; it is tucked in around all edges with enough slack to allow plants to grow normally

Frass – anal excretions of wood-boring insects, often containing sawdust

Gall – a growth that develops on various plants in reaction to the feeding stimulus of some insects and mites

Girdle – encircle, as a tree trunk

Grub – a common term for the juvenile stage of many beetle families, usually somewhat caterpillarlike, often C-shaped

Halteres – modified fore wings of flies; these knobby structures are used for orientation in flight

Herbivore – a plant-eating animal; herbivorous means plant-eating

Hermaphroditic – an animal that is simultaneously male and female

Honeydew – the sweet anal secretion of aphids and scale insects

Insecticide – a chemical used to kill insects

Instar – the stage of an insect between molts; usually only refers to the juvenile form

Larva – the general term for a juvenile insect; plural is larvae

Legume – the general term for a member of the pea family, Leguminosae (e.g., pea, bean, sweet pea)

Maggot – the common term for the juvenile stage of a fly

Metamorphosis – the process of transformation of a juvenile arthropod into an adult

Midge – the common name for some families of small flies

Molt – shedding of the exoskeleton between growth stages

Naiad – the water-dwelling juvenile stage of dragonflies and damselflies

Neem – a fast-growing, broad-leaved evergreen tree, *Azadirachta indica*, native to India

Neem oil – a safe, natural insecticide derived from the neem tree

Nematodes – roundworms in the Phylum Nematoda; all are plant or animal parasites

Nymph – the juvenile stage of insects that undergo gradual metamorphosis; the juvenile stage of the mite

Ocelli – simple eyes of arthropods

Omnivore – an animal that eats both meat and vegetable matter; omnivorous means eating everything

Organophosphate – a large group of synthetic organic pesticides containing phosphorus in addition to hydrogen and carbon

Osmaterium – a defensive organ of swallowtail butterfly caterpillars; this foul-smelling organ is extended from behind the head to repel predators when the caterpillar is threatened

Ovipositor – a tube at the hind end of some female insect species through which eggs are laid; may be spadelike, needlelike, or sawlike

Parasite – an organism that benefits from living, feeding, or reproducing on another organism (a host), while contributing nothing to the benefit of the host; parasites rarely kill their host

Parasitoid – an organism that benefits from living, feeding, or reproducing on another organism, eventually killing the host

Parthenogenesis – the ability to reproduce without benefit of mating, e.g., some aphids have this ability

Pedicel – the short stalk that attaches a spider's thorax to the abdomen

Pedipalps – armlike appendages on the head of a spider; used for touch, as extra legs, or in the case of the male spider, as secondary sexual organs

Pesticide – a chemical used to kill any organism designated as a pest

Petiole – a leaf stalk

Pheromone – a chemical secreted by an animal, especially an insect, that influences the behavior of others of the same species, often to attract members of the opposite sex

Photosynthesis – the chemical process within leaves that combines sunlight, carbon dioxide, and water to produce sugars

Pollinate – to transfer pollen from an anther (male part) to the stigma (female part) of a flower to cause fertilization to occur

Predator – an animal that hunts other animals for food

Prey – an animal that is hunted as food by other animals

Proboscis – mouthparts used to reach into or pierce food

Pupa – the third stage of development of an insect that undergoes complete meta-morphosis in which wings and sex organs develop

Radulae – rasping mouthparts of a slug or snail

Rostrum – the beaklike mouthparts of weevils

Scutellum – the triangular, shieldlike structure behind the head of true bugs

Stabilimentum – the zigzag structure along the radius of the webs of some spiders

Thorax – the middle section of an insect to which wings and legs are attached

Vivipary – the process of giving live birth (e.g., people, some aphids); viviparous refers to an animal that gives live birth

Weevil – the common name of a family of beetles, the Curculionidae

REFERENCES

Acorn, John. *Butterflies of Alberta*. Edmonton, AB: Lone Pine, 1993.

Acorn, John, and Sheldon, Ian. *Bugs of Alberta*. Edmonton, AB: Lone Pine, 2000.

Bird, C. D., et al. *Alberta Butterflies*. Edmonton, AB: The Provincial Museum of Alberta, 1995

Borror, Donald J., and White, Richard E. *Peterson Field Guide to Insects.*   New York, NY: Houghton-Mifflin, 1970.

Buchsbaum, Ralph; Buchsbaum, Mildred; Pearse, John; and Pearse, Vicki. *Animals Without Backbones*, 3d ed. Chicago, IL: The University of Chicago Press, 1987.

Canadian Phytopathological Society and Entomological Society of Canada. *Diseases and Pests of Vegetable Crops in Canada*. Ottawa, ON: Canadian Phytopathological Society and Entomological Society of Canada, 1994.

Carr, Anna. *Rodale's Color Handbook of Garden Insects*. Emmaus, PA: Rodale Press, 1979.

Carson, Rachel. *Silent Spring*. Boston, MA: Houghton-Mifflin, 1962.

Crompton, John. *The Spider*. New York, NY: Nick Lyons Books, 1950.

———*Ways of the Ant*. New York, NY: Nick Lyons Books, 1954.

Delinski, Mike, and Jones, Jim. *Backyard Pest Management in Alberta*. Edmonton, AB: Alberta Agriculture Food and Rural Development, 1994.

Discovery Channel. *Insects and Spiders: An Explore Your World Handbook*. New York, NY: Discovery Channel Publishing, 2000.

Gordon, Deborah. *Ants at Work*. New York, NY: The Free Press, 1999.

Headstrom, Richard. *Spiders of the United States*. Cranbury, NJ: A.S. Barnes and Co., Inc., 1973.

Ives, W. G., and Wong, H. R. *Tree and Shrub Insects of the Prairie Provinces*. Edmonton, AB: Government of Canada, Northern Forestry Centre, 1988.

Johnson, Warren, and Lyon, Howard. *Insects That Feed on Trees and Shrubs*. Ithaca, NY: Comstock Publishing Association, Division of Cornell University Press, 1991.

Mason, Adrienne. *The Nature of Spiders—Consummate Killers*. Vancouver, BC: Greystone Books, Douglas and McIntyre Publishing Group, 1999.

McGavin, George C. *The Pocket Guide to Insects of the Northern Hemisphere*. Hong Kong: Parkgate Books, 1998.

Milne, Lorus, and Milne, Margery. *The Audubon Society Guide to North American Insects and Spiders*. New York, NY: Alfred A. Knopf, 1980.

Olkowski, William; Daar, Sheila; and Olkowski, Helga. *The Gardener's Guide to Common Sense Pest Control*. Newtown, CT: The Taunton Press, 1995.

Opler, Paul A., and Wright, Amy Bartlett. *A Field Guide to Western Butterflies*. 2d ed. Peterson Field Guides. Boston, MA; New York, NY: Houghton-Mifflin, 1999.

Pearman, Myrna, and Pike, Ted. *Naturescape Alberta: Creating and Caring for Wildlife at Home*. Edmonton, AB: Federation of Alberta Naturalists, Red Deer River Naturalists, 2000.

Philip, Hugh, and Mengersen, Ernest. *Insect Pests of the Prairies*. Edmonton, AB: University of Alberta, Faculty of Extension, 1989.

Pyle, Robert Michael. *The Audubon Society Field Guide to North American Butterflies*. New York, NY: Alfred A. Knopf, 1981.

Sargent, Theodore D. *Legion of Night: The Underwing Moths*. Amherst, MA: University of Massachusetts Press, 1976.

Walbauer, Dr. Gilbert. *The Handy Bug Answer Book*. Detroit, MI: Visible Ink Press, 1998.

Zim, Herbert S., and Cottam, Clarence. *A Golden Guide. Insects: A Guide to Familiar American Insects*. Racine, WI: Golden Press, 1987.

WEB SITES OF NOTE

Johnson, D. L. Grasshoppers. Agriculture and Agri-Food Canada, Research Branch, Lethbridge Research Center http://res2.agr.ca/lethbridge/scitech/dlj/johnsond.htm

Government of Alberta Agriculture: http://www.agric.gov.ab.ca/index.html

North Dakota State University: http://www.ndsu.nodak.edu/entomology/

Northern Prairie Wildlife Research Center: http://www.npsc.nbs.gov/index.htm

Provincial Museum of Alberta: http://www.pma.edmonton.ab.ca/natural/insects/intro.htm

University of Saskatchewan: http://www.ag.usask.ca/cofa/departments/hort/hortinfo/pests/index.html

INDEX

In this index, numbers appearing in Roman bold type (e.g., **125**) indicate main entries; italic bold type (e.g., ***44***) indicates illustrations, and square brackets (e.g., [187]) indicate a glossary entry.